THROUGH THE BIBLE
BOOK BY BOOK

by Myer Pearlman

— PART II —
POETRY AND PROPHECY

GOSPEL PUBLISHING HOUSE
Springfield, Missouri

02-0661

⟦ PRINTED ⟧
⟦ IN U·S·A· ⟧

FOREWORD

The reader has, no doubt, watched a grocery salesman fill an order, and noted how well acquainted he was with the sections where the various articles were kept. This homely illustration will serve to describe the purpose of this course, which is to impart a general knowledge of the contents of each book of the Bible so that the Sunday school teacher with his lesson before him, may know from which of the sixty-six "compartments" of the Bible to select his material. This purpose has made necessary the method used in this course, which is not to deal primarily with details, but with the main facts of each book.

CHAPTER I

Job

Theme. The book of Job deals with one of the greatest of mysteries—that of suffering. The question that rings out all through the book is, Why do the righteous suffer? Job, a man described as being perfect, is stripped of wealth, children and health. He bears these afflictions with fortitude. He does not understand the cause of these calamities, but resigns himself to the thought that God sends evil upon men, just as He sends good, and that being God, He has a right to do as He pleases with His own creatures. Therefore men must accept evil uncomplainingly just as they accept good at God's hands. Job's friends argued that, since suffering was the result of sin, and that Job was the most afflicted of all men, therefore Job must be the most wicked of men. Job indignantly denies the charge that he has sinned and carries this denial to the point of self-righteousness. At the conclusion of the discussion between Job and his friends, Elihu speaks up, condemning the former for his self-righteousness and the latter for their harsh condemnation of Job. He then proceeds to explain that God had a purpose in sending suffering to men; that He chastens man for the purpose of bringing him nearer to Himself. God used the afflictions as a trial of Job's character, and as a means of revealing to him a sin of which he had been hitherto unconscious—self-righteousness.

Author. The author of Job is not known. It is believed that Elihu may have written it (32:18-20).

CONTENTS

I.   Satan's Attack on Job (Chs. 1 to 2:10).

Where else is Job mentioned in the Scriptures (Ezek. 14:14; Jas. 5:11)? What is said concerning his character? His prosperity? His piety?

The "sons of God" mentioned in 1:6 are evidently the angels who appeared before God on certain occasions, probably to give a report of their ministry on the earth (Heb. 1:14). As a Judas among the apostles, Satan appears with the angels. Why he had access to God's presence is a mystery, but Revelation 12:10 teaches clearly that he has admittance to heaven, and that there he acts as "accuser of the brethren." (See also Luke 22:31). Notice in verse 7 what Satan says concerning his activity in relation to the world (compare 1 Peter 5:8).

God holds up Job as a perfect God-fearing man, one who has escaped the corruption of the world. Satan admits the fact but impugns Job's motive. His contention is that Job is serving God for the sake of policy, because it brings him prosperity. In assailing Job, Satan attacks also God, for his words carry the insinuation that God is not able to win the unselfish love of man. God, desiring to vindicate His own character and that of His servant, has no alternative but to subject Job to a trial. It is comforting to note that Satan's affliction of the children of God is only by Divine permission. From chs. 1:21 and 2:10 we see that Job justified God's confidence in him.

II.   Job and His Friends. (Chs. 2:1 to 31:40).

We have seen the cause of Job's afflictions from

the Divine viewpoint. We shall now listen to the opinions of his friends concerning the cause of his troubles. It should be remembered that their utterances in themselves are not inspired, for the Lord Himself charged them with error (42:8). It is the **record** of those utterances that are inspired. Though these men said many things that were true, they did not tell the whole truth.

Learn the following points summing up the discourses of Job's friends:

1. They contend that suffering is the result of sin. Therefore if a person is afflicted, it must be taken for granted that he has transgressed.

2. The measure of affliction indicates the degree of sin. They argue that, since Job is the most afflicted of men, he must be the greatest of sinners.

3. They tell Job that if he will repent of his sins God will restore his happiness. They warn him that his trying to justify himself will only delay his restoration.

4. They admit that sometimes the wicked prosper, but they claim that this prosperity is only transient, for it will soon pass away and retribution overtake them.

We may sum up Job's answers to his friends as follows:

1. Job maintains that it is possible for a righteous man to be afflicted. He considers it cruelty on the part of his friends to accuse him of sin because of his afflictions. He himself does not understand God's purpose in afflicting him. He takes it for granted that God, in distributing good and evil, neither regards merit nor guilt, but acts according to His sovereign pleasure. He believes that there are times when a sufferer has a right to justify himself and repine at God's decree.

2. Later Job retracts some of his extravagant assertions, and admits that God generally afflicts

the wicked and blesses the righteous. Still he insists there are exceptions to the rule as, for example when a pious man is afflicted. Because of these exceptions, it is unjust to conclude a man is sinful because of afflictions.

3. He believes that it is our duty to adore God even though suffering calamities not deserved; but we should abstain from harshly judging of those who, when distressed, send forth complaints against God.

III. Elihu's Message (Chs. 32-37).

Elihu's discourse may be summed up as follows:

1. He tells Job that he was wrong in boasting of his integrity (33:8-13), and making it appear that rewards were due to him from God. God is no man's debtor (35:7). However righteous Job may be, he has no claim on God, for all men are sinners in God's eyes.

2. He admits that calamities are punishments for sins committed, but at the same time they are corrective. They might be inflicted on the comparatively most righteous in preference to others. If the object of affliction was attained and the distressed acknowledged his fault, God would bless him with greater happiness than he had before (33:14-33). He then sets forth the majesty and perfection of God in creation, and reproves Job for trying to reason with Him instead of humbling himself and confessing that he was at fault (chs. 36, 37).

IV. Jehovah's Answer to Job (Chs. 38:1 to 42:16).

"God deals with Job only in taking up the discussion. He does not Himself argue with Job, but He gives him the most effective revelations, by which He challenges Job on his own mistaken grounds. He first challenges Job on the mistake of calling the Almighty into question. In judging

God, Job was assuming a power of measurement commensurate with the person and ways he was measuring, namely, the Eternal, the Creator of all things. In Chs. 38, 39, he challenges Job's ability to judge from the standpoint of one acquainted directly and personally with all things in their origins. This silences Job, a man of so brief a span of existence and of original knowledge. God then reveals to Job His amazing skill in fashioning and benevolently governing the most frightful monsters of the ancient world, behemoth and leviathan, the hippopotamus and the crocodile of the Nile, evidently as an illustration of His skill in creating, so to speak, and benevolently governing the most frightful troubles that an all-wise and loving Father may permit the "roaring lion" to inflict. This brings Job out of silence into self-abasing adoration of God. He confesses that what he had learned theoretically before the certainty of Divine wisdom and goodness is now a blessed reality to him, so satisfying and rejoicing his heart that all thought of arguing one's desert under any dispensation of God is forever precluded."— Stevens.

V. Conclusion (Ch. 42:7-17).

The last verses of Job illustrate James 5:11, "Ye have heard of the patience of Job and have seen the end of the Lord, that the Lord is very pitiful and of tender mercy" (i. e., you have seen in the issue of God's dealings with Job, the exercise of His compassion and tenderness).

Psalms

Theme. The book of Psalms is a collection of inspired Hebrew poetry, setting forth the worship and describing the spiritual experiences of the Jewish people. It is the most personal portion of the Old Testament, giving us a revelation of the heart of the Jewish saint, and running over the whole scale of his experiences with God and man. In the historical books we see God speaking **about man,** describing his failures and successes; in the prophetical books we see God speaking **to man,** warning the wicked and comforting the righteous in the light of the future. But in Psalms we see **man speaking to God,** pouring forth his heart in prayer and praise; and speaking about God, describing and exalting Him for the manifestation of His glorious attributes. As the Old Testament saint thus speaks to his God, whatever be his experience, whether of prosperity or adversity, blessing or chastisement, highest ecstasy or deepest despondency, there predominates one note all through his worship—that of praise. He is able to praise God in all circumstances, for His faithfulness in the past is a guarantee of His faithfulness in the future. Also it is this comparison of the past and the future that has been the occasion for the introducing of the prophetical element into the Psalms. For as the scribe or prophet saw the failure of Israel's earthly kingdom and king, he broke forth into inspired utterance concerning the coming of God's glorious kingdom, and of His glorious King—the Messiah. We may thus sum up the theme of the Psalms: God is to be praised in every circumstance of life; and this because of His faithfulness in the past, which is a guarantee of His faithfulness in the future.

Authors. Many of the Psalms are anonymous and the authorship of some are doubtful. The following are the generally recognized authors:

David. He is considered the author of the 71 psalms that bear his name.

Asaph, the conductor of the choral service of the temple in the time of David, and also a seer (1 Chron. 6:39; 2 Chron. 29:30).

Solomon, king of Israel.

Moses, Israel's leader and lawgiver.

Ethan, a singer (1 Chron. 15:19).

Heman, a singer and the king's seer (1 Chron. 6:33; 15:19; 25:5, 6).

Ezra. A scribe, who taught the law to the Jews after the captivity.

Hezekiah, king of Judah.

The sons of Korah, leaders in Israel's worship.

Jeduthun, a director of music in the tabernacle (1 Chron. 16:41, 42).

CONTENTS

In the Hebrew Bible the Psalms are divided into five books, as follows:

Book I. begins with Psalm 1.
Book II. begins with Psalm 42.
Book III. begins with Psalm 73.
Book IV. begins with Psalm 90.
Book V. begins with Psalm 107.

The following classification of the Psalms has been suggested. (Read the Psalms mentioned in this classification. Remember the six main points of the classification.)

1. Psalms of instruction: On the character of good and bad men, their happiness and misery (Ps. 1); on the excellency of the divine law (19, 119); on the vanity of human life (90); duty of rulers (82); humility (131).

2. Psalms of praise and adoration: Acknowledgment of God's goodness and care (23, 103); acknowledgment of His power and glory (8, 24, 136, 148).

3. Psalms of thanksgiving: For mercies to individuals, (18, 34); for mercies to the Israelites generally (81, 85).

4. Devotional psalms: the seven penitential psalms (6, 32, 38, 51, 102, 130, 143); expressive of trust under affliction (3, 27); expression of extreme dejection, though not without hope (13, 77); prayers in time of severe distress (4, 28, 120); prayers when deprived of public worship (42); prayers in time of affliction and persecution (44); prayers of intercession (20, 67).

5. Messianic psalms: 2, 16, 22, 40, 45, 72, 110, 118.

6. Historical psalms: 78, 105, 106.

CHAPTER II

Proverbs

(Read at least ten chapters)

Theme. The book of Proverbs is a collection of short, pithy statements setting forth moral lessons. The purpose of the book is declared from the very beginning; namely, the impartation of wisdom to young men (1:1-7). It is the practical book of the Old Testament, applying the principles of righteousness, purity and godliness to everyday life. The wisdom it teaches is not merely fleshly wisdom and prudence, but a wisdom based on the fear of the Lord (1:7). We may thus sum up its theme: Practical wisdom resting upon and rising out of religious character. "The fear of the Lord is the beginning of wisdom."

Authors. Solomon himself wrote most of the proverbs (1 Kings 4:32; Eccles. 1:13; 12:9). From the reference in places to the "Words of the wise," it is believed that besides his own proverbs, Solomon collected some of those current in his time and incorporated them with his own. The proverbs in the last two chapters were written by Agur and Lemuel, about whom the Bible tells us nothing.

CONTENTS

The following analysis has been given:

I. A connected discourse on the value and attainment of true wisdom (Chaps. 1 to 9).

II. Proverbs, headed "The Proverbs of Solomon" (Chaps. 10:1 to 22:16).

III. Renewed admonitions on the study of wisdom, headed "the words of the wise" (22:17 to 24:34).

IV. Proverbs of Solomon collected by the men of Hezekiah (Chaps. 25-29).

V. The wise instructions of Agur to his pupils, Ithiel and Ucal, and lessons taught to King Lemuel by his mother (Chaps. 30, 31).

Ecclesiastes

Title. The word "Ecclesiastes" means "the preacher." It may have been so called from the fact that Solomon, after his sad experience of backsliding taught publicly his experiences and the lessons learned therefrom.

Theme. In the book of Proverbs we learned about that wisdom which has its source in God. Now, in Ecclesiastes we shall read about that merely natural wisdom, which, apart from God, attempts to seek truth and happiness. Both books were written by Solomon; the first, during the early part of his reign, when he walked with God; the second, during the latter part of his reign when sin had separated him and his Maker. In Proverbs there is heard from his lips a note of joy and contentment as he meditates upon the blessings of divine wisdom; in Ecclesiastes we hear a note of sadness, despair and perplexity as he sees the failure of natural wisdom to solve human problems and secure perfect happiness. After his departure from God (1 Kings 11:1-8), Solomon still retained riches and wisdom. Possessed of these he began his quest for truth and happiness apart from God. The result of this quest is expressed in the ever-recurring phrase "all is vanity" (vanity here means "emptiness, worthlessness"). Solomon learned the following truth which sums up the theme of the book: Without God's blessing, wisdom, position, and riches do not satisfy, but rather bring weariness and disappointment.

Author. Solomon (See 1:1, 16; 12:9).

CONTENTS

I. The Vanity of Human Pleasure and Wisdom (Chaps. 1, 2).

II. Earthly Happiness, Its Hindrances, and Means of Advancement (Chaps. 3-5).

III. True Practical Wisdom (6:1 to 8:15).

IV. The Relation of True Wisdom to the Life of Man (8:16 to 10:20).

V. The Conclusion (11:1 to 12:14).

In reading Ecclesiastes, the student will find together with much sound teaching, much that is at variance with other teaching of the Bible (Read 1:15; 2:24; 3:3, 4, 8, 11, 19, 20; 7:16, 17; 8:15). He should remember that the book is the **inspired record** of the **uninspired utterances** of a natural man, reasoning about human experience and divine providence. In the same way the Bible contains many utterances of wicked men; the **utterances** are uninspired, but the **record** is inspired.

I. The Vanity of Human Pleasure and Wisdom (Chaps. 1, 2).

In 1:1-3, Solomon states the theme of his discourse: the vanity of all human effort and endeavor. All effort is vain, for the mind that would try to search out the secrets of life is not satisfied. Men come and go without discovering the solution of life's problems, but the world still continues to exist with its unsolved mysteries (1:4-18). Thus man's theoretical wisdom fails. Solomon now applies his practical wisdom to the problem of finding happiness (Chap. 2). He tries mirth (vv. 1, 2), wine (v. 3), building (v. 4), wealth and music (vv. 5-8). The result of his quest is stated in verse 11—disappointment. He is filled with despair and weariness as he sees that with all his wisdom, he is not more advanced than a fool in his attempt to solve the problems of life (vv. 12-19). As he considers that the riches which he has labored so hard to accumulate and which have not satisfied him he will have to leave to one who has not worked for them, he is overwhelmed with the sense of the emptiness and worthlessness of effort (vv. 20-23). He comes to the conclusion that the best thing possible for the natural man, is to get the greatest pleasure out of this life, at the same time doing his best to live a moral life (vv. 24, 25).

II. Earthly Happiness, Its Hindrances and Means of Advancement (Chaps. 3-5).

Solomon reasons that in order to attain to happiness, one must rejoice in its blessings and make a righteous use of them (Chap. 3). At the best human happiness is limited, for all human action and effort is restricted by and depends on an unchangeable higher law. In other words, whatever comes, whether good or evil, must come, for everything has its time. Man cannot change this order so he must submit to it and derive all the happiness he can from life (vv. 1-15). Human happiness is restricted because of the natural man's ignorance of the things of the future life. So uncertain to him is the hope of a future life that he wonders whether he is any better than the animals in this respect (vv. 16-21). Because of this uncertainty of a life beyond, there is nothing better for him to do than enjoy the life that now is (v. 22).

He then names the hindrances to happiness (4:1-16), mentioning the personal misfortune of many men (vv. 1-6), the evils of social life (vv. 7-12), and the evils of civil life (vv. 13-16).

He suggests that happiness is to be attained by devotion to the worship of God (5:1-7), by refraining from injustice, avarice and violence (vv.

8-17), and by a temperate enjoyment of the pleasures and treasures of life granted by God (vv. 18-20).

III. True Practical Wisdom (Chaps. 6:1 to 8:15).

True wisdom does not consist in striving after earthly sources of happiness (6:1-12), for even those who possess wealth do not attain to a true lasting enjoyment of them (vv. 1-6), and never escape from the feeling of their emptiness and of the uncertainty of the future (vv. 7-12).

True wisdom consists in a contempt of the world and foolish lusts (7:1-7), in a patient calm and resigned spirit (vv. 8-14), and in an earnest fear of God and a sincere acknowledgment of sin (vv. 15-22).

This wisdom must be preserved in spite of the lusts of the world (7:23-29), in spite of the temptations to disloyalty and rebellion (8:1-8), and in spite of oppressions and injustice (vv. 9-15).

IV. The Relation of True Wisdom to the Life of Man (Chaps. 8:16 to 10:20).

God's dealings with man are sometimes mysterious (8:16 to 9:6), but that should not discourage the wise man from taking an active part in life; rather he should enjoy this life and use it profitably (9:7-10). Though the result of human labor is sometimes uncertain, man should not be discouraged in his search for wisdom (vv. 11-16).

In the presence of the insolence, pride and violence of fortunate fools, the wise man should keep his peace of mind by silence and modesty (9:17 to 10:20).

V. The Conclusion (Chaps. 11:1 to 12:7).

After his reasonings, some of them true, some partially true, and some false, Solomon comes to his conclusions. These represent the very best that the natural man can do, apart from revelation, to attain to happiness and favor with God. They are as follows:

1. Faithfulness in benevolence and in one's calling (11:1-6).

2. A calm and contented enjoyment of this life (11:7-10).

3. The fear of God for young and old in view of a coming judgment (12:1-7).

4. The fear of God and the keeping of His commandments (12:13, 14).

Song of Solomon

Title. The name of this book in the Hebrew Bible is "Song of Songs," so called evidently from the fact that of all Solomon's songs (1 Kings 4:32) it is the greatest.

Theme. The Song of Solomon is a love story, glorifying pure, natural affection, and pointing to the simplicity and sanctity of marriage. That this story has a typical significance may be inferred from the fact that, under the figure of the marriage relation are described Jehovah's love for Israel (Hosea chapters 1-3; Isaiah 62:4), and Christ's love for the church (Matt. 9:15; 2 Cor. 11:2; Eph. 5:25; Rev. 19:7; 21:2.) So then the following theme suggests itself: The love of the Lord for His people as typified by the love of the bride and bridegroom.

Note. In reading this book the student should remember that he is reading an oriental poem, and that Orientals are given to a plainness of speech in the most intimate of matters—plainness of speech foreign and sometimes distasteful to most Occidentals. Delicate and intimate as the language is in many places, it should be noted that there is nothing here that would offend the most modest Oriental. Dr. Campbell Morgan says, "In the first place this was undoubtedly an earthly love-song, but it was very pure and very beautiful. There are men and women who would find indecencies in heaven,—if they ever got there,—but they would take them in their own corrupt souls. To those who live lives of simple purity, these songs are full of beauty as they utter the language of human love; and finally, in spiritual experience, they express the relation of such as have been wooed by God in Christ, and thus have come to love and know Him."

Author. Solomon. (1:1).

CONTENTS

Of all the books of the Old Testament, the Song of Solomon is perhaps the most difficult of interpretation and analysis. In this study we shall limit ourselves to giving a brief outline of the story contained in the song, and of the dialogues between Solomon and his bride. For a devotional study of the Song of Solomon, we would recommend a small inexpensive book by Hudson Taylor, "Union and Communion." This may be obtained from Bethany House Publishing, Minneapolis, MN.

"The story about which this idyl is woven seems to be this: King Solomon visits his vineyard in Mount Lebanon. He comes by surprise upon a beautiful Shulamite maiden. She flees, and he visits her, disguised as a shepherd, and wins her. Soon he comes to claim her as queen. They proceed to the royal palace. Here the poem begins and relates the story of love."—Dr. Haas.

I. The Bride in Solomon's Gardens (Chaps. 1:2 to 2:7).

1. The bride asks for a pledge of love, and praises the bridegroom (1:1-4).

2. She makes a plea to the daughters of Jerusalem not to despise her humble origin, and asks

where she may find the bridegroom. The maidens in chorus reply (1:5-8).

3. Then follows an affectionate conversation between Solomon and his bride (1:9 to 2:7). Solomon speaks, 1:9-11; the bride, 1:12-14; Solomon, 1:15; bride, 1:16 to 2:1; Solomon, 2:2; the bride, 2:3-7.

II. The Bride's Memories (Chaps. 2:8 to 3:5).

1. She recalls her lover's visit one spring (2:8-17).

2. She recalls a dream concerning him (3:1-5).

III. The Betrothal (Chaps. 3:6 to 5:1).

1. The inhabitants of Jerusalem describe the approach of the king and the bride (3:6-11).

2. Then follows a conversation. Solomon, 4:1-5; bride, 4:6; Solomon, 4:7-16a; bride, 4:16b; Solomon, 5:1.

IV. At the Palace (Chaps. 5:2 to 8:4).

1. The bride relates a dream she had concerning Solomon. She dreamed that he had departed, and that in her search for him, she had been harshly treated by the watchmen of the city. In her dream she enquired of the daughters of Jerusalem concerning him, and described his beauty (5:2 to 6:3).

2. Solomon enters and praises her (6:4-9).

3. Dialogue between chorus of maidens and bride; chorus, 6:10; bride, 6:11, 12; chorus and bride alternately, 6:13; chorus, 7:1-5.

4. Solomon enters and praises the bride. 7:6-9.

5. The bride invites her beloved to visit her home (7:10 to 8:4).

V. The Bride's Home (Chap. 8:5-14).

The inhabitants of the country speak, 8:5a; Solomon, 8:5b; the bride, 8:6, 7; her brothers, 8:8, 9; the bride, 8:10, 12; Solomon, 8:13; the bride, 8:14.

CHAPTER III

Isaiah

Theme. Of all the prophetical writings the book of Isaiah is the most beautiful and sublime. In none of the other books do we obtain such a glorious view of the Messiah and of His kingdom. Because of its emphasis of God's grace and His redemptive work in relation to Israel and the nations, the book of Isaiah has been called "The Fifth Gospel," and its author, "the Evangelist of the Old Testament." The two main divisions of the book will aid us in finding its theme. The keynote of the first division (chaps. 1-39) is "Denunciation." As we read this section we hear the rumblings of God's wrath against apostate Israel and against the idolatrous nations surrounding them. In these chapters are prophesied Israel's captivity by the Babylonians, and the tribulation and judgments of the last days. The keynote of the second division (chaps. 40-66) is "Consolation." This section contains prophecies of Israel's return from the Babylonian captivity and of their final restoration and gathering to Palestine in the last days. With these two last-named divisions in mind, we may sum up the theme of Isaiah as follows: The wrath of God resulting in Israel's condemnation and tribulation; the grace of God resulting in their salvation and exaltation.

Author. Isaiah. Isaiah, the greatest of the prophets, was called to the ministry in the reign of Uzziah (Isaiah Ch. 6). His name, which means "salvation of Jehovah," well describes his ministry and message. He prophesied during the reigns of Uzziah, Jotham, Ahaz and Hezekiah, and perhaps during the reign of Manasseh (between 757-697 B. C.). He was a statesman as well as a prophet, for we find him speaking and acting in connection with the public affairs of the nation. Tradition tells us that he was put to death by the wicked Manasseh by being sawed asunder.

Scope. The historical events recorded in Isaiah cover a period of about 62 years from about 760 to 698 B. C.

CONTENTS

Isaiah naturally divides itself into the following three sections:

I. **The condemnatory section,** containing for the most part rebukes of Israel's sins (Chs. 1-35).

II. **The historical section,** containing the account of the Assyrian invasion, and God's merciful deliverance of Jerusalem and Hezekiah's healing (Chs. 36-39). These chapters form a link between the first and last section. They serve as an appendix to the first section, for they record the prophecy of the Babylonian captivity (39:5-8), which was the penalty of Israel's sins condemned in chapters 1-35. Because of this same prophecy, chapters 36-39 form an introduction to the last section which deals with Israel's restoration from captivity.

III. **The consolatory section,** containing words of comfort to chastised Israel and promises of restoration and blessing (Chs. 40-66).

As a basis for our study we shall use the following outline:

I. Prophecies concerning Judah and Jerusalem (Chs. 1-12).

II. Prophecies of judgments on the nations (Chs. 13-23).

III. Prophecies of world judgments ending in Israel's redemption (Chs. 24-27).

IV. Prophecies of judgment and mercy (Chs. 28-35).

V. Invasion and deliverance of Judah (Chs. 36-39).

VI. Deliverance from captivity through Cyrus (Chs. 40-48).

VII. Redemption through suffering and sacrifice (49-57).

VIII. The future glory of the people of God (58-66).

SECTION I: CONDEMNATORY

Before continuing the study of Isaiah let the student read 2 Chronicles 26:1 to 32:33, which will give him the historical background of the book.

I. Prophecies Concerning Judah and Jerusalem (Chs. 1 to 12).

Isaiah begins his prophecy with a vigorous denunciation of the sins of Judah and Jerusalem. In chapter one he strikes the chief keynotes of the entire book. He describes Israel's utter apostasy, an apostasy so great, that were it not for the fact that Jehovah in His grace had left a remnant, the nation would have been exterminated as were Sodom and Gomorrah (vv. 1-9). Apostate Israel has still the form of godliness, but it is simply an empty formality which is a stench in Jehovah's nostrils (vv. 10-15). Then follows a promise of pardon (vv. 16-23), and a promise of restoration through judgment (vv. 24-31).

Chapters 2-4 contain three pictures of Zion: (1) Her exaltation in the last days (2:1-4), after the ushering in of the millennial kingdom. (2) Her present condition of ungodliness, pride and idolatry (2:5 to 4:1). (3) Her purification by the fires of judgment in the last days (4:2-6).

Isaiah continues his denunciation of the sins of Judah and Israel (Ch. 5). The following is a brief summary of chapter 5:

1. In the Parable of the Vineyard is shown Israel's punishment for their failure to fulfill the responsibilities that their blessings and peculiar privileges have laid upon them (5:1-7; compare Matt. 21:23-46).

2. Six woes are pronounced against the nation (5:8-24); against the avaricious rich (vv. 8, 9), against lovers of pleasure (vv. 11, 12), against skeptics (vv. 18, 19), against preachers of false doctrine (v. 20), against the self-righteous (v. 21), against unjust judges (vv. 22, 23).

3. Judgment against the nation is prophesied, in the form of foreign invasion (5:25-30).

Chapter 6 contains the account of Isaiah's call to the ministry.

Notice—

1. The vision—the glory of Christ (compare John 12:41).

2. The effect of the vision—the prophet's consciousness of his own sinfulness (v. 5).

3. His cleansing and his call (vv. 6-8).

4. His message—the judicial blinding of Israel for their willful rejection of the light (vv. 9, 10; compare Matt. 13:14, 15; John 12:39, 40; Acts 28:25-28).

5. His cry "How long?" (v. 11, i. e., how long Israel's blindness would last). The general import of the answer in verses 12, 13 is that this condition will last until there has been a long captivity and exile and a return of a faithful remnant. (See also Matt. 23:39; Luke 21:24; Rom. 11:25).

Chapters 7:1 to 9:7 contain a warning to the king of Judah against forming an alliance with the king of Assyria. The kings of Israel (of the ten tribes) and of Syria had united to invade Judah (7:1) and were planning to place a strange king on the throne of David. Ahaz, fearing for the safety of Judah and for the continuance of the throne of David was preparing to make an alliance with the king of Assyria (2 Kings, Ch. 16). It was at this point that Isaiah was sent to Ahaz to reassure him and to exhort him to trust in Jehovah instead of in the king of Assyria, for the plans of his enemies would be frustrated (7:1-9). Ahaz fears that the line of David will cease if his enemies succeed in capturing Jerusalem (7:6). Therefore Jehovah Himself gives him a sign that the house of David will endure forever. This sign is the birth of a child from a virgin (7:14; compare Matt. 1:21), a child who shall be a light to those Israelites sitting in darkness (9:1, 2), and who shall reign over the house of David forever (9:6, 7).

Chapters 9:8 to 10:4 contain an account of the calamities which Jehovah had sent upon the ten tribes, but which have gone unheeded. These calamities were: foreign invasion (9:8-17), anarchy (9:18-21), and impending captivity (10:1-4).

Chapter 10:5-34 sets forth the Assyrian nation as the instrument of God's judgment upon Judah. The nation upon whom Judah once relied for help (Ahaz sought alliance with Tiglath-Pileser, king of Assyria) has now become a scourge against them. Though Jehovah has commissioned the Assyrian nation to chastise Israel, yet He will judge the former for their pride and arrogance against the One who had used them (10:5-19). Israel will then learn not to put their trust in idolatrous nations (v. 20). However severe Israel's chastisements may be in any age, God in His mercy will always leave a remnant who will form the kernel of a new nation (vv. 20-23). The Jews are not to fear the king of Assyria, who will march upon Jerusalem, for Jehovah will destroy him in a supernatural way (10:24-34; compare 2 Kings, Chs. 18, 19).

As the prophet predicts Jehovah's deliverance of Israel from the Assyrian, his perspective reaches over to the end-time when Israel will be delivered from the antitype of the Assyrian—the Antichrist, and when the Messiah, the Son of Jesse, will establish all Israel in their land, and usher in the millennial kingdom (Chs. 11, 12).

CHAPTER IV

Isaiah (Continued)

II. Prophecies of Judgments on the Nations (Chs. 13 to 23).

The events prophesied concerning the nations in chapters 13 to 23 were fulfilled in a few generations after their prediction. While these prophecies found a near fulfillment by Israel's return from captivity it should be remembered that many of them have a future fulfillment in the last days. The end of prophetic perspective was the millennium, the age bringing Israel's final restoration and subsequent exaltation. In comforting and exhorting the nation, the prophets generally pointed to that far-off event, for, short of this, they could promise no permanent blessing for the nation. With this thought in mind of Israel's final restoration, the prophet, by the inspiration of the Spirit, predicted the **future** in the light of the **present;** i. e., he made present and imminent occurrences a type of future and remote events. For example: when prophesying a **soon-coming** national tribulation, and restoration he would usually look beyond these events into the future and foretell Israel's **final** tribulation and **final** restoration in the last days. The principle which we have just mentioned is known as the "law of double reference," and is found operative in all prophecy in general. The following are the nations mentioned in this section:

1. Babylon (13:1 to 14:27). The destruction of the Babylonian Empire by the Medes and Persians is foretold. This event, to the prophet is a foreshadowing of the destruction of the empire of Antichrist together with its emperor and his inspirer,

Satan (14:9-17). This to be followed by Israel's restoration (14:1-6).

2. Philistia (14:28-32). The Philistines are warned not to rejoice over Israel's invasion by the Assyrians, for such will be their fate also. Verse 32 looks forward to Israel's future restoration.

3. Moab (Chs. 15, 16). The destruction of Moab by the Assyrians is predicted within three years from the time of the utterance of the prophecy. Note reference to last days in 16:5.

4. Damascus, i. e., Syria (Ch. 17). In addressing to Syria a warning of coming judgment, the prophet mentions also her ally, Ephraim (the ten northern tribes). For Israel there gleams a ray of hope of restoration in the last days (vv. 6, 7, 13).

5. Ethiopia (Ch. 18). This chapter describes Ethiopia as in great excitement, sending ambassadors hither and thither, seeking help against the expected Assyrian invader. Isaiah tells these ambassadors to return and quietly watch Jehovah bring to nought the attempt of the Assyrians to conquer Judah.

6. Egypt (Chs. 19, 20). Here are prophesied the judgments of Jehovah upon Egypt—civil war, subjugation beneath an oppressor's yoke and national decadence. Looking forward to the millennial days, the prophet sees Egypt restored, and together with Assyria, forming an alliance with Israel (19:18-25).

7. "The wilderness of the sea," i. e., Babylon (21:1-10). Another prophecy of Babylon's subjugation by the Medes and Persians.

8. Dumah, i. e., Edom (21:11, 12). Edom is seen in great anxiety making inquiry concerning the future. The answer is disappointing but sympathetic.

9. "The valley of vision," i. e., Jerusalem (Ch. 22). The prophet pauses in his denunciations of the heathen nations to utter a warning against

the inhabitants of Jerusalem, who were indulging themselves in luxury and merry-making while the enemy was standing at their door.

10. Tyre (Ch. 23). Isaiah predicts that Tyre shall be laid waste, her commercial glory humbled, her colonies become independent of her, and she herself forgotten seventy years. However there is a promise of her restoration.

III. Prophecies of World Judgments Ending in Israel's Redemption (Chapters 24 to 27).

In chapter 24 the prophet announces a general judgment of the land of Palestine and of the kings and nations of the earth, this to be followed by Israel's restoration.

Chapter 25 records the song that Israel will sing after their restoration, a song celebrating Jehovah's might in destroying the cities of their enemies and His faithfulness in defending Jerusalem. Jehovah will make a feast to all nations in Mount Zion, will remove the covering of spiritual blindness from their eyes, will abolish death, and wipe away all tears. All His enemies of whom Moab is typical and representative, will be destroyed.

Chapter 26:1-19 records Israel's song of praise and testimony after their restoration to Palestine.

Jehovah calls upon the faithful remnant of Israel to hide in the shelter which He has prepared for them to shield them from the great tribulation (26:20 to 27:1). After the tribulation the true vineyard of Jehovah will be protected against the briars and thorns of foreign invasion (27:2-6). Israel's chastisements have been light compared to those of the other nations (vv. 7-11). After their chastisement they will be regathered (vv. 12-13).

IV. Prophecies of Judgment and Mercy (Chs. 28-35).

The above-named chapters contain a series of woes against Samaria, Jerusalem and Edom, interspersed and ending with comforting promises of Israel's restoration and blessing.

1. Woe to the proud, scoffing, spiritual and civil drunken leaders of Samaria and Jerusalem (Ch. 28).

2. Woe to Jerusalem, for the formality and insincerity of her worship (Ch. 29:1-14).

3. Woe to those who attempt to make plans in secret, thinking to hide them from God (29:15-24).

4. Woe to those who go to Egypt for help, instead of trusting the Lord (Chs. 30, 31).

5. At this point the prophet introduces a picture of the millennial kingdom, where justice shall prevail, administered by Jehovah's righteous King, the Messiah (Ch. 32).

6. Woe to the Assyrians for their treacherous dealing with God's people (Ch. 33).

7. Woe to Edom, Israel's implacable foe, and a type of their enemies of the last days (Ch. 34).

8. Israel's glorious restoration to the Holy Land (Ch. 35).

SECTION II. HISTORICAL

V. The Invasion and Deliverance of Judah (Chs. 36 to 39).

This section forms an appendix to chapters 1 to 36 in that it records the fulfillment of the predictions concerning the invasion of Judah by the Assyrians and her deliverance by the Lord (Chs. 8; 10:5-34; 31:5-9). This same section serves as an introduction to chapters 40 to 66 in that it records the prophecy of the Babylonian captivity (39:5-8), thus preparing the way for the promises of restoration.

We may sum up the contents of this section as follows:

1. Sennacherib's invasion (Ch. 36).

2. Hezekiah's prayer and Jehovah's answer (Ch. 37).
3. Hezekiah's sickness and recovery (Ch. 38).
4. Hezekiah's folly (Ch. 39).

SECTION III: CONSOLATORY

VI. Deliverance from Captivity through Cyrus (Chs. 40 to 48).

The above section predicts Israel's deliverance from Babylon by Cyrus, the king of the Persians, who overthrew the Babylonian empire (See also Ezra 1:4). The main thought running through these chapters is: The greatness of Jehovah in contrast with the gods of the nations. The following is a brief summary of their contents:

1. Chapter 40 is the key chapter of this section. The prophet is exhorted to comfort Israel in view of the coming Deliverer (vv. 1-11), Jehovah's greatness (vv. 12-26), and of His power to give strength to the weary (vv. 13-31).

2. The central thought of chapter 41 is: Jehovah's power shown by His ability to predict future events (See vv. 1-4, 22, 23).

3. Jehovah has predicted Israel's **temporal** deliverance through Cyrus. Now in Chapters 42:1 to 43:13 He promises **spiritual** deliverances through His Servant, the Messiah.

4. This spiritual deliverance is to be effected by the blotting out of Israel's sins by the grace of God. This is the message of chapters 43:14 to 44:23.

5. In chapters 44:24 to 45:25 we are given a description of the mission of Israel's deliverer—Cyrus, king of the Persians, who is here a type of the Messiah. It should be noted that Cyrus was surnamed and commissioned by the Lord 150 years before his birth (45:1-4).

6. Chapters 46, 47 describe God's judgments on Babylon, Israel's captor and oppressor.

7. The argument of chapter 48 is as follows: Since Jehovah, one hundred and fifty years before, had predicted the restoration of Israel from Babylon through a heathen prince, the exiles could not claim that it was the power of idols that caused Cyrus to liberate them.

VII. Redemption through Suffering and Sacrifice (Chs. 49 to 57).

The above-named chapters describe the Author of Israel's spiritual redemption—the Servant of Jehovah. The main theme is: redemption through suffering. The following is a brief summary of the chapters:

1. The ministry of Messiah, the Servant of Jehovah (Ch. 49).

2. The humiliation of the Messiah by rebellious Israel (Ch. 50).

3. Encouragement to the faithful remnant of Israel to trust in God both for deliverance from their long Babylonian exile and from their present dispersion (Chs. 51:1 to 52:12).

4. The rejection, humiliation, death, resurrection and exaltation of the Messiah (Chs. 52:13 to 53:12).

5. Israel's repentance for their rejection of the Messiah to be followed by their restoration (Ch. 54).

6. The result of Israel's restoration—the call of all nations to faith in the Messiah (Chs. 55, 56).

7. Comforting promises to the faithful remnant in Israel, and denunciations of the wicked of the nation (Ch. 57).

VIII. The Future Glory of the People of God (Chs. 58 to 66).

The prevailing thought of the above division is: the establishing of God's universal kingdom and its triumph over every form of evil. The following is a brief summary of its contents:

1. An exhortation to practical religion as opposed to mere formality (Ch. 58).

2. An exhortation to Israel to forsake their sins which have separated between them and God (59:1-15). Seeing the helplessness of Israel in their iniquity and the inability of any of their leaders to help them, God Himself, in the person of the Messiah, comes to rescue them from their sins and from their enemies, after which He makes an everlasting covenant with them and puts His Spirit within them (59:16-21).

3. Then follows a picture of Israel's glory after their affliction (Ch. 60).

4. Chapter 61 sets forth the twofold commission of the Messiah to bring Gospel mercy at His first coming and judgment on unbelievers and comfort to Zion at His second coming.

5. The appointing of intercessory prayers for Zion's restoration (Ch. 62).

6. Chapter 63:1-6 stands by itself. It gives us a vivid picture of the Messiah as the Avenger of His people at His second coming.

7. Chapters 63:7 to 64:12 record the intercessory prayers of the faithful Jewish remnant. They remind Jehovah of His mercy and grace to their nation in the past, and plead for that same mercy and grace in the forgiveness of their sins and in the restoration of their land.

8. In His answer to the prayer of His people (Chs. 65:1-16), Jehovah justifies His dealings in relation to His people. Because of Israel's apostasy He has cast them off and turned to a people that did not seek Him neither were called by His name—the Gentiles. In Israel, Jehovah distinguished two classes: His own servants and the apostates. Only the former will be delivered while the latter will perish.

9. Isaiah closes his prophecy with a glorious prophecy of the coming of the millennial kingdom

(65:17 to 66:24). People will grow old like the patriarchs; they will enjoy the possession of houses and vineyards (65:17-24). Even the nature of ferocious beasts will be changed (65:25).

Religion will become spiritual and universal and mystic cults will disappear and their adherents will be punished (66:1-5). Zion's population will be marvelously increased and the people will rejoice (66:6-14). After judging those nations that have gathered themselves against Jerusalem (vv. 15-18), Jehovah will send His servants to preach the glad tidings to them (v. 19). Those who once persecuted Israel will transport them to Palestine (v. 20), and from among those who were once enemies of the true religion, Jehovah will choose ministers to serve before Him (v. 21), as representatives of a worship which will be universal (vv. 22-24).

CHAPTER V

Jeremiah

Theme. Isaiah and Jeremiah both carried messages of condemnation to apostate Israel. But whereas the tone of Isaiah is vigorous and severe, that of Jeremiah is mild and gentle. The former carries an expression of Jehovah's wrath against Israel's sin; the latter, an expression of His sorrow because of the same. In rebuking Israel, Isaiah dipped his pen in fire; Jeremiah dipped his in tears. Isaiah, after his denunciation of Israel's iniquity, burst forth into raptures of joy at the prospect of the coming restoration. Jeremiah had a glimpse of the same happy event, but it was not sufficient to dry his tears or dispel the gloom of his sorrow for Israel's sinfulness. Because of this last fact Jeremiah has been known as "the weeping prophet." The following will serve as the theme of his book; Jehovah's unchanging love toward His backslidden people and His sorrow for their condition.

Author. Jeremiah. He was the son of Hilkiah, a priest of Anathoth in Benjamin. He was called to the ministry while still young (1:6), in the thirteenth year of King Josiah, about seventy years after the death of Isaiah. Later, probably because of persecution of his townspeople and even of his own family (11:21; 12:6), he left Anathoth and came to Jerusalem. There and in other cities in Judah, he ministered for about forty years. During the reigns of Josiah and Jehoahaz, he was allowed to continue his ministry in peace, but during the reigns of Jehoiakim, Jehoiachin, and Zedekiah he suffered severe persecution. In the reign of

Jehoiakim he was imprisoned because of his boldness in prophesying the desolation of Jerusalem. During the reign of Zedekiah, he was arrested as a deserter, and remained in prison until the taking of the city, at which time he was released by Nebuchadnezzar and allowed to return to Jerusalem. On his return, he tried to dissuade the people from returning to Egypt to escape what they believed to be an impending danger. They ignored his appeals and migrated to Egypt taking Jeremiah with them. In Egypt he continued his efforts to turn the people to the Lord. Ancient tradition tells us that, angered by his continued warnings and rebukes, the Jews put him to death in Egypt.

Scope. From the 13th year of Josiah to the early part of the Babylonian captivity, covering a period of about 40 years.

CONTENTS

Because of lack of chronological order in the prophecies of Jeremiah, it is difficult to give a satisfactory analysis of them. We suggest the following:

I. Jeremiah's Call and Commission (Ch. 1).

II. General Message of Rebuke to Judah (Chs. 2 to 25).

III. More Detailed Message of Rebuke and Judgment and of Restoration (Chs. 26 to 39).

IV. Messages after Captivity (Chs. 40-45).

V. Prophecies Concerning Nations (Chs. 46-51).

VI. Retrospect: the Captivity of Judah (Ch. 52).

Before continuing the study of Jeremiah, read 2 Kings Chs. 22 to 25, which will give the historical background of the book.

I. Jeremiah's Call and Commission (Ch. 1).

We shall notice as the contents of this chapter:

1. Jeremiah's origin—from a priestly family living in Benjamin (v. 1).

2. The time of his ministry—from the reign of Josiah to the beginning of the Babylonian captivity (vv. 2, 3).

3. His call—to be a prophet to the nations (vv. 4, 5).

4. His enduement—inspired by Jehovah (vv. 6-9).

5. His commission—to prophesy the fall and restoration of nations (v. 10).

6. His message to Israel—to prophesy the coming Babylonian invasion (symbolized by the seething pot) and the imminence of that event (symbolized by the almond tree vv. 11-16).

7. Jeremiah's encouragement — protection against persecution (vv. 17-19).

II. General Message of Rebuke to Judah (Chs. 2 to 25).

The following are the contents of this section:

1. Jeremiah's first message to Judah (2:1 to 3:5). In this message Jehovah reviews Israel's past, reminds them of their past blessings and deliverances, rebukes them for their present backsliding, self-righteousness and idolatry, and pleads with them to return to Him.

2. Jeremiah's second message (3:6 to 6:30). Jehovah reminds Judah of the fact that He cast the ten tribes out of His sight for their idolatry, and that instead of taking warning from the fate of the ten tribes, they have continued in the same sins (3:6-10). The Lord then appeals to the Northern kingdom (in captivity) to repent, expressing His love for them and, making promises of restoration in the last days (3:11 to 4:2). He then addresses to Judah an exhortation to repentance, and this appeal failing, He pronounces upon them the judgment of the Babylonian invasion (4:3 to 6:30).

3. Discourse in the temple gate (Chs. 7-10). The theme of this discourse is as follows: because of Israel's formality in worship, their idolatry, their violation of God's law, their rejection of His messengers, their universal and incurable backsliding, Jehovah will give the land of Judah over to invasion and will scatter the inhabitants among the nations.

4. The message on the broken covenant (Chs. 11, 12). The occasion of this message was the finding of the book of the law in the reign of Josiah (2 Kings 22:8-23). The main theme of this message is as follows: God's curse upon Judah because of the violation of the Mosaic covenant.

5. The message of the linen girdle (Ch. 13). By the symbolic actions of the prophet's putting on a girdle, burying it by the banks of the Euphrates, and then unearthing it, is typified Jehovah's election of Israel to be His own people, His rejection of them for their rebelliousness, and His humbling of them by the Babylonian captivity.

6. Prophecies on the occasion of a drought in Judea (Chs. 14, 15). Jeremiah, recognizing this drought as a judgment of God makes intercession for the people (Ch. 14). But so incurable has become Israel's iniquity that intercession will no longer avail, even though Moses and Samuel—two of Israel's greatest intercessors—were to plead for them (15:1-10). Though the whole nation is to be delivered over to judgment, yet God will preserve a remnant, of whom Jeremiah is representative (15:12-21).

7. The sign of the unmarried prophet (Ch. 16:1 to 17:18). Jeremiah is commanded not to marry, as a sign of the imminence of God's judgments, the awfulness of which would make the single state preferable to the married. As further signs of the same event he is commanded not to mourn (v. 5), for since God had taken away peace from His peo-

ple only a false consolation could be given; he is
also commanded not to engage in legitimate mer-
rymaking, for in view of impending judgment,
such would be a mockery (v. 9). Through the calamities prophesied in these chapters, there gleam
some rays of hope for Israel (16:15-21).

8. The message concerning the Sabbath (17:19-
27). The Sabbath was a sign of God's covenant
between Him and the children of Israel (Ex. 31:16,
17). So then a violation of the Sabbath day would
be equivalent to a violation of God's covenant, and
would bring the penalty prophesied by Jeremiah
(Ch. 17:27).

9. The sign of the potter's house (18:1 to
19:13). God's power to deal with the nations according to His sovereign will is symbolized by the
potter's molding of vessels. God can mold Israel
as a potter can a vessel. If they are rebellious He
can mar them; if they repent He can remake them
(Ch. 18). Since Israel persist in their apostasy
God will cast them away. This is typified by the
breaking of a potter's vessel (19:1-13).

10. Jeremiah's first persecution (19:14 to
20:18). Jeremiah's prediction concerning the destruction of Jerusalem angers a priest's son by
the name of Pashur, who himself had been prophesying Jerusalem's safety (20:6). He vents his anger on the prophet by inflicting on him the pain-
ful punishment of the stocks. For this act of
persecution, Jehovah pronounces judgment upon
Pashur, at the same time repeating the prophecy
of the Babylonian captivity. The latter part of
chapter 20 reveals the effect of this persecution
on the timid nature of Jeremiah. He was tempted
to seal his lips and refrain from prophesying. But
the fire within was stronger than the fire without;
so he continued to preach (20:9).

11. The message to king Zedekiah (Chs. 21,
22). This was uttered in response to Zedekiah's in-

quiry concerning Nebuchadnezzar's invasion. Evidently when inquiring of the Lord he had not the slightest intention of heeding the counsel or commandments that might be given, for the response to his inquiry is a message of severe judgment upon him (vv. 1-7). Jehovah then addresses the people offering to such who are willing to listen to Him, a means of escape from the coming destruction (21:8-10). He then offers a way of escape to the royal house from the coming judgment—an escape that can be affected by their executing judgment and righteousness (21:11-14). As examples of the sureness of divine retribution, Jehovah reminds Zedekiah of the fate of the three kings preceding him; probably repeating messages that had been delivered to them: Shallum, or Jehoahaz, (22:11); Jehoiakim (22:18); Jeconiah, or Jehoiachin (22:24).

12. Jehovah has been speaking about the unrighteous kings of Israel. He now promises the coming of the righteous King, the Messiah who shall restore Judah and Israel (23:5-6). Chapter 23 contains for the most part a denunciation of the false prophets, who, instead of exhorting the people to repentance by the warnings of impending judgment, were lulling them into a false security with promises of peace and safety.

13. The sign of the figs (Chap. 24). Under the figure of good and bad figs is shown the future of those Jews of the first deportation in the reign of Jeconiah and those of the final captivity in the reign of Zedekiah. The former would be restored and replanted in Palestine; the latter would be given up to the sword and would be scattered among the heathen.

14. Chapter 25:1-14 contains a prophecy of the seventy years captivity of Judah, this to be followed by the destruction of Babylon, Israel's oppressors.

15. Under the figure of a wine-cup of fury
is set forth God's judgment of the nations (25:15-
38).

III. More Detailed Messages of Rebuke and Judgment and of Restoration (Chapters 26 to 39).

The following are the contents of this section:

1. Jeremiah's repetition of his message concerning the destruction of Jerusalem endangers
his life. However he is protected from the fury
of the priests and the people by the judges of the
city (Ch. 26).

2. Under the figure of yokes is set forth the
subjugation of Judah and the surrounding nations
by Nebuchadnezzar, king of Babylon (Chs. 27, 28).
This message, which was given in the reigns of
Jehoiakim and Zedekiah, was directed against
those false prophets who were encouraging the
people to rebel against Nebuchadnezzar, and who
were promising a speedy return of the exiles of
the first deportation.

3. The message to the captives of the first deportation (Ch. 29). This letter was written to
instruct the exiles to prepare to make their home
in Babylon for a period of seventy years, and to
warn them not to give heed to those prophets who
were falsely predicting a speedy return.

4. After contemplating Israel's present captivity and coming deliverance, the prophet gazes
into the future and sees Israel delivered from the
final tribulation at the end of the age, restored
to their land, under Messiah the son of David,
cleansed from their sins and enjoying the blessings
of the New Covenant that God will make with
them (Chs. 30, 31).

5. As a sign of the coming restoration of the
land, Jeremiah is led by the Lord to purchase a
portion of land from one of his relatives (Ch. 32).

Upon seeing the condition of the city surrounded by the Chaldeans, Jeremiah's faith seems to fail concerning the promise of restoration. Whereupon in his perplexity he goes before the Lord in prayer (vv. 16-25). Jeremiah is assured that nothing is too hard for the Lord, who is able to pardon and purge Israel's iniquity and restore them to their land (vv. 26-44).

6. Chapter 33 continues the theme of Israel's restoration. Their final restoration is assured by Jehovah's promise (vv. 1-14), by Jehovah's Branch, the Messiah (vv. 15-18), and by Jehovah's faithfulness in keeping His covenant (vv. 19-26).

7. Chapter 34 contains a prophecy of Zedekiah's captivity and a denunciation of the people of Jerusalem for the breaking of a covenant. The law of Moses required that Hebrew slaves be released after seven years' service. This command had long been violated. It seems that Jeremiah's preaching and fear of the coming captivity had stirred the people's consciences to the extent of making them willing to sign a covenant to release their slaves. But when Nebuchadnezzar withdrew his armies for a time, and the danger of invasion seemed to be past, the people showed the shallowness of their motives by breaking their agreement. Since they had made captives of others, they, too, would become captives, decreed Jehovah.

8. The message concerning the Rechabites (Ch. 35). The Rechabites were descended from Hobab, the brother-in-law of Moses. They were Kenites and migrated with Israel to Canaan (Num. 10:29; Judges 1:16; 4:11-17; 5:24; 1 Sam. 15:6). They are held up as an example to the Jews, and the disobedience of Jehovah's divine law by the latter is contrasted with the Rechabites' unwavering obedience to the simple rules of living laid down by their ancestor.

9. The writing of Jeremiah's prophecies in the

days of Jehoiakim (Ch. 36). In a final attempt to bring Israel to repentance the Lord commanded Jeremiah to commit to writing all the prophecies he had uttered since the beginning of his ministry, in order that the same might be repeated to the people. Jehoiakim's treatment of this writing was typical of the attitude of the nation at large and a sealing of their doom.

10. Jeremiah's imprisonment (Ch. 37). The Chaldean army that was besieging Jerusalem raised the siege in order to meet the armies of the king of Egypt who was advancing to attack them. Zedekiah, fearing lest, in the event of the Chaldeans overcoming the king of Egypt, they should return and besiege Jerusalem, sent to inquire of Jeremiah concerning the matter (v. 3). Jehovah's answer was that the Chaldeans would certainly return and destroy the city. Jeremiah taking advantage of the departure of the besieging army, prepared to visit his native town, and in so doing was arrested as a deserter to the enemy. When the Chaldeans returned, as Jeremiah had previously prophesied, Zedekiah again came to inquire of him. Again he was met with a discouraging reply. His treatment of Jeremiah (v. 21) shows how honest reproof in the end gains more than flattery.

11. While Jeremiah was still in the court of the prison (37:21) a deputation came to Zedekiah asking that Jeremiah be put to death because of the prophet's persistence in preaching that Jerusalem was doomed to destruction and that only those surrendering to the Chaldeans would escape. This message, they claimed, was weakening the courage of the people. Jeremiah was then cast into a dungeon, but was transferred to the prison court on the intercession of Ebedmelech. There he had a secret interview with Zedekiah in which he assured that monarch that

his only chance of escape was his surrender to the Chaldeans (Ch. 38).

12. Chapter 39 records the fall of Jerusalem, the final captivity of Judah, the death of Zedekiah, the deliverance of Jeremiah by Nebuchadnezzar, and the reward of Ebed-melech.

CHAPTER VI

Jeremiah (Continued)

IV. Messages After the Captivity (Chaps. 40 to 45).

1. Offered the choice of going to Babylon with the prospect of worldly advancement or returning to his own people, Jeremiah nobly chose the latter. He returned and dwelt with Gedaliah whom the king of Babylon had appointed governor of the land. To the latter was brought news of a plot against his life, which he unwisely ignored (Ch. 40).

2. The plot of which Gedaliah had been notified was carried out and he was assassinated by Ishmael, the son of Nethaniah. The latter gathered the remnant of the people that were in Mizpah and prepared to flee to Moab, but his attempt was frustrated by Johanan and the captains of the forces that were with him. Fearing that the Chaldeans would take vengeance on the remnant for the murder of Gedaliah, Johanan prepared to lead the people to Egypt (Ch. 41).

3. Though the leaders had made up their mind as to their plans they inquired of the Lord as to what course they should pursue. Jehovah's answer was that their safety depended on their staying in Judea, and that their going to Egypt would mean their destruction (Ch. 42).

4. Since this advice was contrary to their plans and intentions, the leaders ignored it and in the face of Jehovah's prohibition they went into Egypt, taking the remnant of the people with them. While in Egypt Jeremiah foretold by a type the conquest of Egypt by Nebuchadnezzar (Ch. 43).

5. Chapter 44 contains Jeremiah's last message to Judah. The remaining prophecies of the

book concern the Gentiles. It was not long before the remnant had yielded to the lure of Egyptian idolatry, and when rebuked for this by Jehovah, brazenly expressed their intention of sacrificing to the Queen of Heaven, i. e., Venus. Because of this attitude on their part, their destruction is prophesied and as a sign of this, invasion of Egypt by Nebuchadnezzar is predicted.

6. Chapter 45 contains a message to Baruch delivered about 18 years before the fall of Jerusalem. The occasion for the message is stated in verses 1-3. The persecution arising from his writing and reading of the prophecies of Jeremiah in the reign of Jehoiakim had evidently discouraged him (v. 3), and perhaps had thwarted some of his cherished plans and ambitions (v. 5).

Jehovah tells him that since He is bringing evil on the whole land of Judah, Baruch is not to seek any advancement or good for himself there, but rather to rejoice in the fact that his life will be protected wherever he goes.

V. Prophecies Concerning the Nations (Chs. 46 to 51).

The following nations are addressed:

1. Egypt (Ch. 46). This chapter contains three distinct prophecies. The defeat of Pharaoh-necho, king of Egypt, by the king of Babylon at the battle of Carchemish, on the Euphrates (vv. 1-12). It was on his way to Babylon that this Egyptian king encountered and slew King Josiah (2 Chron. 35:20-24). The conquest of Egypt by the king of Babylon (vv. 13-26). The restoration of Israel (vv. 27, 28).

2. Philistia and Tyre (Ch. 47). The invasion of these countries by Nebuchadnezzar is foretold.

3. Moab (Ch. 48, compare Isaiah Chs. 15, 16). Judgment in the form of invasion and devastation by the Chaldeans is pronounced upon Moab for the following reasons: their trusting in their works

and treasures (v. 7); their living in ease and luxury (v. 11); their rejoicing at Israel's misfortunes (v. 27); their magnifying themselves against the Lord (v. 42). Their restoration in the last days is prophesied (v. 47).

4. Ammon (49:1-6). Ammon is to be judged for seizing the land of Gad when the ten tribes went into captivity (2 Kings, Ch. 17), when Judah not Ammon was heir to that territory (v. 1); also for her pride of land and riches and her carnal security (v. 4). This same nation assisted the Chaldeans in their attacks on Judah (2 Kings 24:2) and later exulted at her fall (Ps. 83:1-7). For Ammon restoration is promised in the latter days (v. 6).

5. Edom (49:7-22). Jehovah pronounces the sentence of utter destruction upon a nation which always was Israel's implacable enemy (Num. 20:18; Ezek. 25:12-14; Ch. 35; Amos 1:11; Obadiah, Ch. 1).

6. Damascus, capital of Syria (49:23-27). This city was invaded by Nebuchadnezzar five years after the destruction of Jerusalem.

7. Kedar and Hazor (49:28-33). Kedar was the country of the Arabs; Hazor, a neighboring country.

8. Elam (49:34-39). The judgment of dispersion is pronounced against this nation, perhaps for helping Nebuchadnezzar against Judah. Their restoration is promised in the latter days, which promise may have found a partial fulfillment on the day of Pentecost when Elamites heard the Gospel (Acts 2:9).

9. Babylon (Chs. 50, 51, compare Isaiah Chs. 13, 14, 47). In the preceding chapters we learned that Jehovah used Babylon as a scourge upon Israel and upon the surrounding nations. But the fact of her being used by Jehovah will not save her from judgment for her sins (Jer. 27:7). Com-

pare God's dealings with the Assyrian nation (Isa. 10:4-34; 37:36-38). For the record of the fulfillment of the prophecies found in Jeremiah 50, 51 read Daniel Ch. 5. Remembering what was said concerning the law of double reference, we may regard the fall of Babylon as typical of the overthrow of Antichrist's kingdom and his capital, possibly a rebuilt Babylon. With Jeremiah 50, 51 compare carefully Revelation Chs. 17, 18.

VI. Retrospect: the Captivity of Judah (Chap. 52).

The account of the destruction of Jerusalem recorded in 2 Kings Chs. 24, 25; 2 Chron. Ch. 36; and Jeremiah Ch. 39 is repeated here. It is fitting that the record of the event that drew so many tears from Jeremiah and which well-nigh broke his heart, form the conclusion of his book.

Lamentations
(Read the book)

Theme. The book of Lamentations is an appendix to the prophecy of Jeremiah, recording the keen, heart-breaking sorrow of the prophet for the miseries and desolations of Jerusalem resulting from her siege and destruction. The grief and lamentations expressed in Jeremiah's prophecy find their culmination here; the river of tears that flowed there becomes a torrent in this book. The leading object of the book was to teach the Jews to recognize God's chastening hand in their calamities and to turn to Him in sincere repentance. Jeremiah's mournful dirge has been taken up by the Jewish nation, for they chant this book every Friday at the wailing place in Jerusalem, and they read it in the synagogue on the fast of the ninth day of August, the day set apart to mourn over the five great calamities that had befallen the nation. We shall sum up the theme of Lamentations as follows: The desolations of Jerusalem, the result of her sins, and a chastisement from a faithful God to lead her to repentance.

Author. Jeremiah.

CONTENTS

We shall give here the outline suggested by Mr. Robert Lee of London. The book consists of five poems.

I. First poem: the city represented as a weeping widow. Chap. 1.

II. Second poem: the city represented as a veiled woman mourning midst the ruins. Chap. 2.

III. Third poem: the city represented as, and by, the weeping prophet mourning before Jehovah the Judge. Chap. 3.

IV. Fourth poem: the city represented as gold dimmed, changed, degraded. Chap. 4.

V. Fifth poem: the city represented as a suppliant pleading with the Lord. Chap. 5.

This book is still used by the Jews today to breathe out their sorrow at the sufferings and dispersion of Israel. The Lamentations are still read yearly to commemorate the burning of the Temple. Every Friday, Israelites, old and young, of both sexes, gather at the Wailing Place in Jerusalem, near the southwest corner of the old temple grounds, where an ancient wall 52 yards in length and 56 feet in height, is still revered as a memorial of the sanctuary of the race. Writes Dr. Geikie: "It is a touching sight to watch the line of Jews of many nations, in their black gabardines, as a sign of grief, lamenting aloud the ruin of that House whose very memory is still so dear to their race, and reciting the sad verses of Lamentations and suitable Psalms, amid tears, as they fervently kiss the stones. On the ninth of the month Ab, nearly our July, this dirge, composed about six hundred years before Christ, is read aloud in every synagogue over the world.

CHAPTER VII

Ezekiel

Theme. Ezekiel prophesied in Babylon during the entire period of his ministry, which began seven years before the destruction of Jerusalem, and which ended about fifteen years after that event. Like that of Isaiah his message was one of denunciation and consolation. "The central point of Ezekiel's predictions is the destruction of Jerusalem. **Before** this event his chief object was to call to repentance those living in careless security; to warn them against indulging the hope that, by the help of the Egyptians, the Babylonian yoke would be shaken off (17:15-17); and to assure them that the destruction of their city and temple was inevitable and fast approaching. **After** this event, his principal care was to console the exiled Jews by promises of future deliverance and restoration to their land; and to encourage them with assurance of future blessings."—(Angus-Green). We shall sum up the theme as follows: The departure of God's glory from Israel in prospect of coming judgment; and the return of His glory in prospect of future restoration.

Author. Ezekiel. Like Jeremiah, Ezekiel was a priest as well as a prophet. He was carried captive together with King Jehoiachin by Nebuchadnezzar about ten years before the destruction of Jerusalem. He made his home at Tel-Abib in Babylon. There he ministered to the exiles who, for the most part, resisted his words, clinging to the false hope of a speedy return. Tradition tells us that he was put to death by one of the exiles whom he had rebuked for idolatry.

Scope. The historical events recorded in this book cover a period of 21 years from about 595 to 574 B. C.

CONTENTS

I. The Prophet's Call (Chs. 1-3).

II. The Fate of Jerusalem and the Nation (Chs. 4-24).

III. Prophecies Against the Nations (Chs. 25-32).

IV. The Restoration of Israel (Chs. 33-48).

I. The Prophet's Call (Chs. 1 to 3).

We shall notice here:

1. Ezekiel's vision, (chap. 1). Like that of Isaiah, Ezekiel's call was preceded by a vision of the glory of the Lord (Compare Isaiah Ch. 6). The living creatures mentioned in this chapter are the cherubim, an order of angelic beings whose ministry seems to be, in relation to mankind, the guardianship and vindication of God's holiness (See Gen. 3:24; Ex. 25:18-22; Num. 7:89; 1 Sam. 4:14; 2 Sam. 6:2; 1 Kings 8:6, 7; 2 Kings 19:15; Psalm 18:10; 80:1; 99:1; Rev. 4:6-8).

2. His commission and message (2:1—3:9). As in the case of Isaiah, Ezekiel's message was one of condemnation to a disobedient people.

3. His responsibility (3:10-21). He is appointed as a watchman over the house of Israel, with a solemn warning against neglect of duty.

4. His second vision of the glory of the Lord (3:22-27). Ezekiel was not to begin immediately his ministry of preaching, but was to refrain from speaking till so instructed by the Lord. He was to abide in his house until he received from the Lord the revelations concerning Israel's fate.

II. The Fate of Jerusalem and of the Nation (Chs. 4 to 24).

1. Ezekiel has been commanded by the Lord

to be silent until instructed to prophesy (3:26, 27);
but though silent concerning oral messages, he is
commanded to speak to the nation by means of
symbolic actions, or signs (Chs. 4-6), as follows:

(a) By a tile and an iron pan Ezekiel acts out
the siege of Jerusalem (4:1-3).

(b) To signify the punishment that Israel was
to bear for the period of 390 years in which they
had sinned (from Jeroboam's establishment of idolatry till the 23rd year of Nebuchadnezzar); and
Judah's punishment for her forty years' iniquity
(beginning at Josiah's covenanting, 2 Kings 23:3-
27, and ending at the events recorded in Jeremiah
52:30), Ezekiel lies on his side a day for each year
of that period of idolatry and sin (4:4-8).

(c) To signify the famine that is to prevail
during the siege, he is to eat his bread by weight
and drink his water by measure (4:9-17).

(d) By the sign of the cutting of the prophet's
hair is symbolized the destruction of the people of
Jerusalem by famine, pestilence, and the sword
(5:1-17).

2. A series of messages predicting desolations
upon the land and judgments upon the people
(Chs. 6, 7).

3. A vision of the destruction of Jerusalem
(Chs. 8-11).

(a) One of the causes of its coming destruction—the idolatry of its inhabitants (Ch. 8).   The
beast worship of Egypt (v. 10); the immoral rites
of the worship of Tammuz (v. 14); Persian sun-
worship (v. 16).

(b) A vision of the slaughter of the people and
the sealing of a faithful remnant (Ch. 9).

(c) A vision of the scattering of the altar fire
over Jerusalem, perhaps symbolic of the burning
of the city (Ch. 10).

(d) The departure of God's glory from Jerusalem—a sign of coming judgment (Ch. 11).

4. By the signs of Ezekiel's removing as a fugitive and his partaking of his food as if in time of famine, is set forth the nearness of Judah's captivity (Ch. 12). Then follows a denunciation of the prophets who falsely predict peace and a speedy return from captivity (Ch. 13), and of those leaders who with insincere motives inquire of the Lord concerning the same matter (Ch. 14).

5. Israel's worthlessness is set forth under the figure of a burning vine (Ch. 15), and her faithlessness under the figure of a harlot (Ch. 16).

6. In the parable of the great eagle is shown the punishment of Zedekiah's treachery in breaking his covenant with Nebuchadnezzar, and in calling the aid of Egypt in rebelling against him (Ch. 17).

7. Jehovah's vindication of Himself against the charge that He was punishing the present generation for the sins of their fathers (Ch. 18).

8. A lamentation over the fall of the house of David (Ch. 19).

9. A review of Israel's history illustrating their faithlessness and Jehovah's longsuffering and faithfulness, and teaching that His fidelity is a guarantee of their future restoration, even though that restoration must come through the purging fires of tribulation (Ch. 20).

10. By the sign of the sighing prophet and the sword of God, is again repeated the warning of Jerusalem's coming destruction by Nebuchadnezzar (Ch. 21). Notice the prophecy of the overthrowing of the throne of David until Messiah come (vv. 26, 27).

11. An enumeration of Jerusalem's sins, which will bring her through the fiery furnace of affliction for her purification (Ch. 22).

12. Israel's and Judah's apostasy and punishment is set forth under the parable of Aholah and

Aholibah, the two faithless and adulterous women
(Ch. 23).

13. Jerusalem is compared to a boiling pot and
her inhabitants to the bones and meat within,
producing a vile scum; this is typical of the seething wickedness of the city (Ch. 24:1-4). The destruction of her temple, the pride of the nation,
is symbolized by the Lord's taking away of Ezekiel's wife (24:15-20).

III. Prophecies Against the Nations (Chs. 25 to 32).

Like Isaiah and Jeremiah, Ezekiel has a message for the nations surrounding Israel (Compare
Isaiah 13-23 and Jeremiah 46-51). It is a message
of judgment based in most cases on their treatment of Judah. The following nations are mentioned:

1. The Ammonites (Ch. 25:1-7). (a) The cause
of judgment: their rejoicing at Judah's calamity
(v. 3). (b) Form of judgment: Invasion and desolation.

2. Moab (25:8-11). (a) Cause of judgment:
their insinuation that Judah was no better than
the heathen who worshiped idols—an indirect
thrust at Jehovah (v. 8). (b) Form of judgment:
invasion.

3. Edom (25:12-14). (a) Cause of judgment:
their attitude toward Judah in the day of their
calamity (v. 12). (b) Form of judgment: retribution at the hands of Israel.

4. Philistia (25:15-17). (a) Cause of judgment: their taking advantage of Judah's calamity
to vent their old hatred upon them (v. 15). (b)
Form of judgment: destruction.

5. Tyre (Chs. 26-28). (a) Cause of judgment:
rejoicing over Jerusalem's fall, in expectation of
profiting by their loss (26:2); the blasphemous ex-
ultation of her prince (28:2, 6). Note: in 28:12-
19, Ezekiel looks past the prince of Tyre, to the

one who is empowering him—Satan, the god and prince of this world. (b) Form of judgment: invasion and destruction by Nebuchadnezzar and perpetual desolation.

6. Zidon (28:20-24). (a) Cause of judgment: they were a pricking brier to the house of Israel; i. e., they were the means of ensnaring the Israelites into sin and the instruments for punishing them (Compare Num. 33:55). (b) Form of judgment: slaughter and pestilence.

7. Egypt (Chs. 29-32). (a) Cause of judgment: the arrogance and pride of her king (Ch. 31); their promising help to Israel and then failing them in the emergency (29:6, 7). (b) Form of judgment: slaughter, captivity, abasement among the nations, foreign oppression, destruction of idols, and permanent loss of native ruler.

IV. The Restoration of Israel (Chs. 33 to 48).

Up to this point Ezekiel's message had been that of impending doom for the city and captivity for the people. But now that his predictions have been fulfilled the element of consolation predominates in his prophesying.

1. Ezekiel's commission is renewed, and after the arrival of the news of the capture of Jerusalem, he is allowed to speak plainly to the people instead of preaching by means of signs and symbols.

2. A rebuke of the false shepherds of Israel who drive and oppress the flock, and the promise of the coming of the true Shepherd who will gather and feed the lost sheep of the house of Israel (Ch. 34).

3. The punishment of Israel's enemies, of whom Edom is representative, the gathering of Israel, their complete restoration to a restored land of Palestine and their conversion (Chs. 35, 36).

4. By the vision of the valley of dry bones is symbolized Israel's national death and resurrection; however, the two kingdoms of Judah and Israel are

yet to be united under King David (either David res-
urrected or the Messiah Himself, the descendant of
David) and as a whole bound to Jehovah by an everlasting covenant (Ch. 37).

5. Chapters 38 and 39 record the attack of the
Gentile nations on Israel after they have been restored to Palestine. Read in connection with these
chapters Zech. 12:1-4; 14:1-9; Matt. 24:14-30; Rev.
14:14-20; 19:17-21. Many scholars believe that Russia is referred to in 38:2; Meshech (Moscow), Tu-
bal (Tobolsk). The truth of this opinion is strongly
confirmed when we learn that the words "the chief
prince" should be translated "prince of Rosh"; and
Rosh, we learn from a great Hebrew scholar, probably refers to Russia.

6. The glory of Jehovah which departed from
Israel before their captivity, now returns to abide
in the Millennial temple, of which we find a detailed description in chapters 40-48.

CHAPTER VIII

Daniel

Theme. The book of Daniel is, for the most part, a prophetical history of Gentile world-power from the reign of Nebuchadnezzar to the coming of Christ. The prophets in general emphasize God's power and sovereignty in relation to Israel, and they reveal Him as guiding the destinies of His chosen people throughout the centuries until their final restoration. Daniel, on the other hand, emphasizes God's sovereignty in relation to the Gentile world-empires, and reveals Him as the One controlling and overruling in their affairs, until the time of their destruction at the coming of His Son. "The vision is that of the overruling God, in wisdom knowing and in might working; of kings reigning and passing, of dynasties and empires rising and falling, while God enthroned above rules their movements" (Campbell Morgan). The theme of Daniel may be summed up as follows: God revealed as the One controlling the rise and fall of the kingdoms of this world until their final destruction, and establishing His own kingdom.

Because of its many visions, the book of Daniel has been called "The Revelation of the Old Testament."

Author. Daniel was of the tribe of Judah and probably a member of the royal family (1:3-6). While yet a youth he was carried captive to Babylon in the third year of King Jehoiakim (2 Chron. 36:4-7), and eight years before Ezekiel. Together with three other young men he was stationed at the court of Nebuchadnezzar for special training in the learning of the Chaldeans. There he attained to one of the highest ranks in the kingdom, a position which he retained under the Persian rule, which succeeded the Babylonian. He prophesied during the whole of the captivity, his last prophecy being delivered in the reign of Cyrus, two years before the nation's return to Palestine. Because of his unblemished life amid the corruptions of an oriental court, he is one of those mentioned by Ezekiel as outstanding examples of piety. The same prophet bears witness to his wisdom (Ezek. 28:3).

Scope. From Nebuchadnezzar to Cyrus, covering a period of about 73 years from 607 to 534 B. C.

CONTENTS

I. Introduction: Daniel and his companions (Ch. 1).

II. God's control of the empires of the world in relation to their development and to His kingdom (Chs. 2-7).

III. Daniel's vision in relation to the fortunes of God's people (Chs. 8-12).

I. Introduction: Daniel and his companions (Ch. 1).

Daniel's resolve. Daniel was a truly great man. As concerning personal holiness, he lived a blameless life amid the sensuality of an oriental court; as concerning wisdom and knowledge, he excelled the greatest of Babylon's wise men; as concerning position, he occupied one of the highest stations of the kingdom. Verse 8 reveals the secret of his success: "But Daniel purposed in his heart that he would not defile himself . . ." It was customary among the Babylonians to throw a small part of food and drink on the earth as an offering to the gods, in order to consecrate to them the whole feast. For Daniel to have partaken of such food would have been to sanction idolatry; therefore, like Moses and Joseph he "chose rather to suffer affliction with the people of God than to enjoy the pleasures of sin for a season." As in the case of Joseph, Daniel and his companions were well rewarded for their faithfulness.

II. God's control of the nations of the world in relation to their development and to His kingdom (Chaps. 2 to 7).

1. In response to an unexpressed desire on the part of Nebuchadnezzar to know the future of his great empire, God gave him a dream, which interpreted by Daniel, gave that monarch a revelation of the rise, progress and fall of Gentile world-power during that period described by Christ as "the times of the Gentiles" (Luke 21:24). By the "times of the Gentiles" we mean that period of time during which world dominion is in the hands of the Gentiles instead of the Jews, and during which the Jews are under Gentile rule. This period began with the captivity, 606 B. C., and will end with the coming of Christ. The succession of world empires is set forth under the figure of a gigantic image composed of various metals. In the diminishing value of the metals composing the image may be seen the deterioration of world empires in relation to their character of government. The following is the interpretation of Nebuchadnezzar's dream:

(a) The head of gold represents the empire of Nebuchadnezzar, Babylon (606-538 B. C.). The power of Nebuchadnezzar was absolute, he could do what he willed (Dan. 5:19). His empire was **a unit**.

(b) The breast and arms of silver represent the inferior empire of Medo-Persia (538-330 B. C). This kingdom was inferior to the first, for its monarch depended on the support of the nobility, and could not do what he willed, as shown by the inability of Darius to release Daniel (6:12-16). This empire was **dual,** composed of the empires of Media and Persia.

(c) The belly and thighs of brass represent the less valuable empire of Greece (330-30 B. C.). "The government of Alexander was a monarchy supported by the military aristocracy that was as weak as the ambitions of its leaders." This empire was later divided into **four parts** (7:6; 8:8).

(d) The legs of iron, and the feet and toes, part iron and part clay, represent the Roman empire (B. C. 30 till the return of Christ). Here is represented a still inferior form of government, in that the emperor of Rome was elected and his power depended on the good will of the people. This empire will, in the last days, be divided into **ten parts.** The mingling of the iron with the clay in the ten toes suggests a further deterioration of this government into that of a democratic monarchy where the monarch carries out the will of the people (2:41-43).

(e) The stone cut out without hands falling on the feet of the image signifies the coming of Christ at a time when the Roman empire will have been restored, His destruction of Gentile world-power, and the setting up of His own kingdom.

2. Nebuchadnezzar's image, the refusal of the three Jews to worship, and their deliverance from the fiery furnace (Ch. 3).

3. Nebuchadnezzar's tree vision, his abasement and his restoration (Ch. 4).

4. Daniel's personal history under Belshazzar and Darius (Chs. 5, 6).

(a) Under Belshazzar: his interpretation of the writing on the wall (Ch. 5).

(b) Under Darius: his deliverance from the lions' den (Ch. 6).

5. The vision of the four beasts (Ch. 7). This

chapter treats of the same subject as the second chapter—the rise and fall of Gentile power. In chapter 2 the empires are viewed from the **political** viewpoint, in relation to their deterioration in form of government; in chapter 7 they are viewed from the **moral** viewpoint in relation to their fierce and destructive characters as expressed by their symbolization as wild beasts. In chapter two the vision was adapted to the viewpoint of Nebuchadnezzar who saw superficially the world-empire as a splendid human figure and the kingdom of God as a mere stone at first. In chapter seven the vision was adapted to the viewpoint of Daniel, who saw the empires in their true character of wild beasts, and who from the first saw the superiority and triumph of the kingdom of God. The following is the interpretation of the vision:

(a) The lion signifies Nebuchadnezzar's empire. Verse 4 may have reference to Nebuchadnezzar's experience recorded in 4:16-34.

(b) The bear symbolizes the Medo-Persian empire. Its being raised on one side is expressive of the superior strength of the Persian empire. The three ribs in its mouth represent three kingdoms this empire subdued—Lydia, Egypt, Babylon.

(c) The leopard represents the Grecian empire. The wings denote the rapidity of its conquests. The four heads signify the four divisions into which the empire was divided after the death of its ruler.

(d) The undescribed beast represents the strong and terrible Roman empire. The ten horns signify the ten kingdoms into which it will be divided in the latter days. Out of these horns comes another—Antichrist. The days of these ten kingdoms will witness the coming of Christ in power who will destroy that great world system and its ruler. Revelation, chapters 13 and 19 should be read in this connection.

III. Daniel's visions in relation to the fortunes of God's people (Chs. 8 to 12).

1. The vision of the ram and the goat (Ch. 8). The following is a brief interpretation of this vision:

(a) The two-horned ram represents the empire of Medo-Persia.

(b) The he-goat signifies the Grecian empire which destroyed the Medo-Persian.

(c) The notable horn between the eyes of the he-goat represents Alexander the Great, the ruler of the Grecian empire.

(d) The four horns coming up after the breaking of the great horn represent the four divisions of Alexander's empire after his death.

(e) The little horn coming out of one of the divisions of Alexander's empire (vv. 9-14; 23-27). Some scholars believe that the predictions concerning the little horn were fulfilled in a Syrian king named Antiochus Epiphanes, who in his fierce persecution of the Jews, defiled their sanctuary and attempted to abolish their religion. Others contend that the time element mentioned in verses 17, 19, 23 removes the fulfillment of the prophecy to the end of the age when Antichrist, of whom Antiochus is but a shadow, shall appear.

2. The vision of the seventy weeks (Ch. 9). On learning from the prophecies of Jeremiah that the seventy years of Israel's captivity were accomplished, Daniel went before the Lord in intercession for his people. While praying an angel was sent to reveal unto him the future of Israel. The nation was indeed to be restored from captivity, but that restoration was not the final one. A period of seventy weeks (more literally, "seventy sevens") was to intervene before the consummation of Israel's history (v. 24). These weeks are not weeks of days but prophetic weeks of years. By careful calculation scholars have found that this period

sets the exact date of Christ's first coming and
fixes the time of the reign of Antichrist. The seventy weeks are divided into three periods (See
9:25, 26):

(a) Seven weeks, or forty-nine years. The
entire period of the weeks was to be reckoned
from the decree to rebuild Jerusalem which decree was given in March, 445 B. C. during the
reign Artaxerxes (Nehemiah 2:1-10). The period
of the 49 years probably represents the time occupied in the building of the wall as mentioned
in 9:25.

(b) The 62 weeks, or 434 years. After the
period of the 49 years, 62 weeks, or 434 years—
483 years in all—were to elapse before Messiah's
coming. Reckoning from March, 445 B. C., the
year of the decree to build Jerusalem, making al-
lowance for the different calendar used in those
days, and allowing for leap years, students have
calculated that the 483 years, or the 69 weeks, ended in April, 32 A. D., the exact month and year in
which Christ entered Jerusalem as the Messiah
Prince (Matt. 21:1-11). After this period Messiah was to be cut off.

(c) Thus far we have accounted for 69 weeks
out of the 70, 483 years out of the 490. There remains yet one week or 7 years to be fulfilled. Between the 69 weeks and the last week is a gap,
during which period time is not reckoned in relation to Israel. This gap is filled by the church
age, which age was not revealed to the prophets.
The last week or seven years mentioned in verse
26 does not find its fulfillment until the appearing
of Antichrist at the end of the age. Verse 27 af-
firms that a certain ruler will make a covenant
with the Jews for a period of the 7 years, which
covenant he will break after three and a half years,
and after which he will wage war against the religion of the Jews. This implies that the latter

three and a half years of the seven will be a time of tribulation for the Jewish people. The book of Revelation mentions a like period of three and a half years (stated under different symbolic numbers; see Rev. 11:2, 3, 9; 12:6, 14; 13:5), which period it associates with the reign of Antichrist, the tribulation of the Jewish people and the pouring out of God's judgments in the earth—a period which is to be followed by Christ's coming and the restoration of Israel. Thus we see that the last week of the seventy still awaits fulfillment.

3. Daniel's last vision (Chs. 10-12). These chapters contain a prophetic history of God's chosen people from the time of Darius until the coming of the Messiah. The following are the contents of these chapters:

(a) Daniel's vision of the glory of the Lord (Ch. 10).

(b) The wars between two of the four divisions of Alexander's empire—Egypt and Syria, the kingdom of the South, and the kingdom of the North (11:1-20). Palestine had a definite relation to these struggles between these countries for she was a buffer state.

(c) A prophetic description of Antiochus Epiphanes, the great Syrian persecutor of the Jews, and a type of Antichrist (11:21-35).

(d) Daniel now looks from Antiochus, the type, to Antichrist, the antitype, and describes the latter (11:36-45).

(e) The Great Tribulation and the deliverance of the Jewish people (12:1).

(f) The resurrection (12:2, 3).

(g) The last message to Daniel (12:4-13). He is told that the words he has written are closed and sealed unto the time of the end; i. e., the visions are not to find their complete interpretation until the end of the age. The prophecies he had written were not for himself (compare 1 Pet. 1:10-

12), but for those living at the end-time, at which time the wise—i. e., those having spiritual wisdom would understand (v. 10; compare Matt. 24:15). With Daniel's instructions contrast those of John in Rev. 22:10.

CHAPTER IX

Hosea

The book of Hosea is the first of the minor prophetical books. These books are termed "minor" not in relation to their importance but in relation generally to their length, in which respect they stand in contrast to the writings of the Major Prophets.

Let the student read 2 Kings 14:23 to 15:31, which will give him the historical background of the book.

Theme. The book of Hosea is a great exhortation to repentance addressed to the ten tribes, during the fifty or sixty years preceding their captivity. Their cup of iniquity had been fast filling. The kings and priests were murderers and debauchees; idolatrous priests had lured the people away from the worship of Jehovah; when in trouble the government resorted for help either to Egypt or to Assyria; the people in many cases were imitating the moral vileness of the Canaanites; they were living in a careless security, interrupted only in times of danger by a feigned repentance; above all, God and His Word were forgotten. These sins of the nation in her condition of separation from God is summed by the prophet as the sin of spiritual adultery, and is illustrated by his own experience in his marrying an unchaste woman and her forsaking him for another lover. Israel's sin is more grievous than that of the nations surrounding her. The sins of the latter are offences committed by those who have had no relation to Jehovah. Israel's sin is that of unfaithfulness to her husband Jehovah, who delivered her from Egypt, provided for her, and with whom she entered into sacred vows of obedience and faithfulness at Mt. Sinai. But instead of putting this adulterous wife to death as the law prescribed, Jehovah manifests love toward her that is above the human—He receives her again unto Himself. The following will serve as the theme of Hosea: Israel, the unfaithful wife abandoning her husband; Jehovah, the compassionate Husband receiving her again.

Author. Hosea was a prophet of the northern kingdom (the ten tribes). He prophesied at the same time as Amos in Israel and Isaiah and Micah in Judah. His prophetic ministry, lasting about 60 years, is the lengthiest of all the prophets.

Scope. The historical events referred to in the book of Hosea cover a period of about 60 years from about 785 B. C. to the time of the captivity of the ten tribes.

CONTENTS

I. Separation: Israel, the Unfaithful Wife of Jehovah (Chs. 1-3).

II. Condemnation: Israel, the Sinful Nation (Chs. 4 to 13:8).

III. Reconciliation: Israel, the Restored Nation (Chs. 13:9 to 14:9).

I. Separation: Israel the Unfaithful Wife of Jehovah (Chs. 1 to 3).

1. Hosea's marriage to an unchaste woman (Ch. 1). God often spoke to His people through signs and symbolic actions (compare Jeremiah 13:1-11; 19:1-13; Chs. 27, 28; Ezek. Ch. 4). These signs were necessary in order to provide forceful illustrations for the prophet's message and to arouse the people's attention at times when they refused to give heed to the spoken word. Hosea is commanded to marry an unchaste woman as a sign

to the people that they as the wife of Jehovah,
have been unfaithful to their vows of fidelity. This
union must have shocked the people; and this it
was intended to do, in order that, on their enquir-
ing concerning this union, they might discover that
they themselves were represented by Hosea's unfaithful wife. "Moreover the prophet's motive in
marrying the woman was a pure and lofty one.
He was to give her his name and his protection,
and lift her out of her former life of moral degra-
dation unto the same high plane on which he lived.
But why does he do this? Is it not clear that
Hosea's marriage with this unchaste woman illus-
trates Jehovah's marriage with an unchaste people? Did Israel have anything more to commend
her to God's love and care when He took her to
Himself, than this woman when Hosea married
her (Deut. 9:4-6; Isa. 51:1, 2)?"—Dr. Gray. The
children of this union were given names symbolical
of God's judgments on the nation:

(a) Jezreel ("God will scatter"): a sign of the
doom of both the house of Jehu and of the nation
of Israel. Jezreel was the royal city of Ahab and
his ancestors. Here Jehu exercised his greatest
cruelties. It was here that the Assyrians routed
the armies of Israel.

(b) Lo-ruhammah ("unpitied"): a sign of
God's withdrawal of mercy from His people.

(c) Lo-ammi ("not my people"): a sign that
God would disclaim His people.

2. The restoration of Israel in the last days
and their union with Judah under the Messiah
(1:10, 11).

3. Israel, the unfaithful wife (Ch. 2). Chapter
two gives us a more expanded view of Israel's guilt
and misery and their final restoration. It contains
an explanation of the signs of chapter one. After
enjoying Jehovah's goodness and protection, Israel deserted Him and joined herself in an idola-

trous union to Baal (vv. 1-8). Because of this Jehovah will strip her of all His gifts and bring her land into desolation (vv. 9-13). Through tribulation Israel will return to her husband Jehovah to whom she will be betrothed forever (vv. 14-23).

4. Jehovah the faithful husband (Ch. 3). As a sign of Jehovah's mercy and love toward His people Hosea is commanded to take back his unfaithful wife who had deserted him (v. 1). It seems that she had been sold in slavery from whence Hosea redeemed her (v. 2). But before full restoration to conjugal rights there were to intervene many days during which she was to live free from impurity (v. 3) In like manner Israel is to remain for a long period free from all idolatry until the time of her restoration to full covenant privileges under Messiah (vv. 4, 5). This last prophecy has been remarkably fulfilled in the Jewish people. For hundreds of years they have been without a king or prince, without priest or sacrifice, and since the return from the Babylonian captivity, they have been free from idolatry.

II. Condemnation: Israel the Sinful Nation (Chaps. 4 to 13:8).

In the first three chapters Jehovah spoke of Israel's unfaithfulness to Him by means of the sign of Hosea's marriage. In chapters 4-13 He speaks in plain language to the nation, mentioning the different sins that went to make up Israel's apostasy. This section consists of many discourses that do not lend themselves readily to analysis. We may sum up the theme of this section as follows: Israel's sin and guilt and Jehovah's exhortation to them to repent.

III. Reconciliation: Israel, the Restored Nation (Chs. 13:9 to 14:1).

1. Though Israel has destroyed herself through

sin and died as a nation, God will bring about her
national resurrection (13:9-16. Compare Ezek.
Ch. 37).

2. As one teaching a child to pray, Jehovah
gives Israel the very words she should use in returning to Him (14:1-3).

3. As soon as Israel is ready with words of repentance Jehovah is ready with words of blessing
and restoration (14:4-9).

Joel

Theme. The occasion for Joel's prophecy was
an unusually severe invasion of destructive insects
—locusts—which devastated the land, destroying
the harvests, and bringing on a general famine.
The prophet sees in this calamity a visitation from
God and refers to it as a type of the final world-
judgment—the day of the Lord (1:15). Like many
of the other prophets, Joel predicts the future in
the light of the present, regarding a present and
imminent event as a type of a future event. Therefore he sees in the invasion of the locusts a foreshadowing of the coming invasion of the Assyrian
army (Ch. 2:1-27; compare Isaiah Chs. 36, 37).
Looking still farther into the future he sees the
invasion by the locusts and Assyrians as typical of
the final invasion of Palestine by the confederated
armies of Antichrist. Taking the "Day of the
Lord" as the central thought, and remembering
that the same expression is used as referring to the
invasion of the locusts and the Assyrians, we shall
sum up the theme of Joel as follows: The Day of
the Lord, seen as immediate (in the invasion of the
locusts), as imminent (in the coming Assyrian invasion), and as future (in the final invasion).

Author. Little is known concerning Joel. It
is believed that he prophesied during the time of
Joash, king of Judah (2 Kings, Ch. 12).

CONTENTS

The first section (Ch. 1) describes the literal plague of locusts. The terribleness of the plague may be judged of by the following description of the locusts: "The land over which their devastating hordes have passed at once assumes the appearance of sterility and dearth. Well did the Romans call them 'the burners of the land,' which is the literal meaning of the word 'locust.' On they move, covering the ground so completely as to hide it from sight, and in such numbers that it often takes three or four days for the mighty host to pass by. When seen at a distance this swarm of advancing locusts resembles a cloud of dust or sand, reaching a few feet above the ground as the myriads of insects leap forward. The only thing that momentarily arrests their attention is a sudden change of weather, for cold benumbs them while it lasts. They also keep quiet at night swarming like bees on the bushes and hedges until the morning sun warms and revives them and enables them to proceed on their devastating march. They 'have no king' nor leader, yet they falter not, but press on in serried ranks, urged in the same direction by an irresistible impulse, and turn neither to the right nor to the left for any sort of obstacle. When a wall or house lies in their way, they climb straight up, going over the roof to the other side and blindly rush in at open doors and windows. When they come to water be it a puddle or river, a lake or an open sea, they never attempt to go round it, but unhesitatingly leap in and are drowned; and their dead bodies floating on the sur-

face form a bridge for their companions to pass
over. The scourge thus often comes to an end,
but it as often happens that the decomposition of
millions of insects produces pestilence and death."
—Van Lennep.

The contents of the second section may be
summed up as follows:

1. The invasion of the Assyrians typified by
the locust invasion (2:1-11). The Assyrians were
like locusts because of their number and destructive influence.

2. A call to repentance (2:12-17).

3. A promise of deliverance (2:18-27).

In chapters 2:28 to 3:21 the prophet projects
his vision into the time of the end, and he sees:

1. The outpouring of the Spirit upon the Jewish nation (2:28, 29). This prophecy had a partial
fulfillment on the Day of Pentecost.

2. The signs preceding the Lord's coming
(2:30-32).

3. Armageddon and the judgment of the nations (3:1-16).

4. The restoration of Israel (vv. 17-21).

Amos

Theme. The message of Amos is that of judgment to come and restoration to follow. It will
be noted that there is a certain sameness in the
themes of many of the prophets. This is explained by the fact that there was one predominating
cause that brought forth their message, namely,
national sin; therefore their message was in most
cases one of condemnation. But while they had a
message of rebuke for the nation at large, they had
also a message of consolation and restoration for a
faithful remnant. Amos views the sin of Israel in
relation to the great privileges granted them, and
shows that because of the great privileges that

were theirs and because of their failure to walk worthy of the favors Jehovah had bestowed upon them, their punishment will be greater than that of the heathen who have not had the same advantages as they (3:2). The theme of Amos may be stated as follows: The setting forth of the sins of a privileged people, whose privileges brought them great responsibility and whose failure under that responsibility brought them a judgment according to the light they had received.

Author. Amos was a native of Tekoa, about six miles south of Bethlehem, inhabited chiefly by shepherds, to which class he belonged, being also a gatherer of sycamore fruit. He had not been officially ordained as a prophet, neither had he attended the school of the prophets; his only reason for preaching was a divine call (7:14, 15). His ministry was primarily to the Ten Tribes, although he had also a message for Judah and the surrounding countries. He prophesied during the reigns of Uzziah, king of Judah (2 Chron., Ch. 26) and of Jeroboam II, king of Israel (2 Kings 14:23-29), from 60 to 80 years before the captivity of the Ten Tribes. "Bethel was the principal scene of his preaching, perhaps the only one. When he had delivered several addresses there Amaziah, the chief priest of the royal sanctuary, sent a message to the king, who seems not to have been present, accusing the preacher of treason, and at the same time ordered the latter to quit the realm. Evidently there was some reason to fear that the oppressed poor might be stirred up to revolt against their lords and masters. The threats of coming judgment would disturb many hearers. The denunciations of cruelty and injustice would awaken many echoes. Yet the priest's language evinces all the contempt which a highly placed official feels towards an interfering nobody, a fellow who thinks he gains a precarious livelihood by prophesying

(7:10-17). On reaching home Amos doubtless put
into writing the substance of his speeches."—J.
Taylor.

CONTENTS
    I. Judgment on the Nations (Chs. 1, 2).
    II. Judgment on Israel (Chs. 3 to 9:6).
    III. The Restoration of Israel (9:7-15).

I. Judgment on the Nations (Chaps. 1, 2).

Israel and Judah are included in this denunciatory message against the nations, for Jehovah
is seen as the Judge of all nations administering
impartial judgment. Notice how each of these
messages begins: "For three, . . . yea, for four."
This is a figurative way of declaring that God does
not act immediately in judgment; but that He
waits in order to give every nation the chance
of repentance." Dr. Campbell Morgan sums up
briefly the sin of each nation as follows:
    1. The sin of Syria: cruelty (1:3-5).
    2. The sin of Philistia: slave trade (1:6-8).
    3. The sin of Phoenicia: slave agents in spite
of covenant (1:9, 10).
    4. The sin of Edom: determined and revenge-
ful unforgiveness (1:11, 12).
    5. The sin of Ammon: cruelty based on cupidity
(1:13, 15).
    6. The sin of Moab: violent and vindictive
hatred (2:1-3).
    7. The sin of Judah: Jehovah's laws despised
(2:4, 5).
    8. Israel: corruption and oppression (2:5-16).

II. Judgment on Israel (Chaps. 3 to 9:6).

The judgments are set forth in three discourses (3:1 to 6:14) and by five visions (7:1 to
9:6).
    1. The three discourses, each beginning with
the words "hear this word":

(a) The theme of the first discourse (Ch. 3), is as follows: Israel's ingratitude for God's love and favor and their failure under responsibility calls for punishment (3:1-3); which the prophets announced, not at random, but by God's commission which they cannot but fulfill (vv. 4-8). From this judgment only a remnant (v. 12) will escape (vv. 9-15).

(b) The theme of the second discourse (Ch. 4). Because of the oppression of the nobles (4:1-3) and the general idolatry of the nation (vv. 4, 5) they have been chastised (vv. 6-11). Because these chastisements have been unheeded Israel is to prepare to meet their God in the last and worst judgment of all (vv. 12, 13).

(c) The theme of the third discourse (5:1 to 6:14). Impending judgment may be averted by seeking Jehovah (5:1-15). For those who scornfully wish to see the day of Jehovah, it will come in all its awfulness and terror (5:16-20); because of the nation's deserting of God's true service in imitation of their fathers in the wilderness they will be led into captivity (vv. 21-27); woe to those who live in carnal security as though that captivity were not impending (Ch. 6).

2. The five visions of judgment.

(a) The locusts (7:1-3). These were typical of the Assyrians who were constantly ravaging Israel. At the intercession of the prophet, Jehovah promises that all Israel shall not be utterly destroyed.

(b) The burning up of the deep (7:4-6). This probably refers to the drying up of the waters and a consequent drought.

(c) The plumbline (7:7-9). As a sign that judgment is about to be meted out according to righteousness. This last message brought persecution upon the prophet from Israel's high priest (7:10-17).

(d) The basket of summer fruit (8:1-3). This was symbolical of Israel's ripeness for judgment. Then follows a message (8:4-14) the theme of which is as follows: because Israel has despised the Word of God, God will bring on a famine of that same Word.

(e) The Lord standing upon the altar (9:1-6). The Lord is seen commanding to smite and slay, showing that the order is being given for the judgment to begin.

III. The Restoration of Israel (Ch. 9:7-15).

1. The dispersion of Israel is for their sifting and purification (vv. 7-10).

2. After that is accomplished the Davidic kingdom will be re-established (v. 11).

3. Then the whole nation Israel will be the head of the nations (v. 12).

4. The land of Palestine will prosper (vv. 13, 14).

5. And Israel will inherit it forever (v. 15).

CHAPTER X
Obadiah

(Read the book of Obadiah)

Theme. The theme of Obadiah can be clearly seen at the first reading of the book. It is: Edom's great sin—violence against Judah; their punishment—national extinction. "Edom was descended from Esau, and Israel, from Jacob. The antagonism between them is patent throughout the Bible. In the book of Genesis occurs a simple and yet most suggestive declaration, 'The children struggled within her' (Gen. 25:22, 23). From that hint of the consciousness of Rebekah the story of the antagonism continued. The antagonism obtained in the family circle and continued when the descendants of each had expanded into a nation. The Edomites were a proud, bitter, resentful people, ever seeking an oportunity to harm Jacob's descendants. Israel and Edom were perpetually at war. When Nebuchadnezzar captured Jerusalem, Edom rejoiced over Israel's downfall, and cruelly took part in the plundering and massacre (Ps. 137:7). In days gone by God had commanded His people to treat Edom kindly (Deut. 23:7), but now their atrocious conduct had filled up their cup of iniquity, and sentence of condemnation and annihilation was passed upon them. After Israel's restoration, Cyrus, king of Persia, overcame them, slaughtering thousands of them. They received another crushing defeat by the Jews under the Maccabees (109 B. C.). The antagonism of Edom and Judah came to a head in the time of Christ. Jesus Christ was a Jew, a descendant of Jacob; Herod, an Edomite, a descendant of Esau. To him Christ never spoke

(Matt. 14:6-9; Luke 23:9). After the siege of Jerusalem, 70 A. D., the Edomites are lost sight of." Verses 10-14 indicate that the book was written after the destruction of Jerusalem.

Author. Absolutely nothing is known concerning Obadiah. There are many of that name mentioned in the Old Testament.

CONTENTS

I. The Sin of Edom: Pride (vv. 1-9).

II. Their Greatest Sin: Violence against Judah in the Day of Their Calamity (vv. 10-14).

III. Their Punishment: National Destruction (vv. 15-21).

Jonah

Theme. The book of Jonah is peculiar among the prophets in that it contains no direct message to Israel, the message of the prophet being addressed to the Ninevites. But though not directly stated, there is a great lesson in this book for the Jewish nation; namely, that God is the God, not only of the Jews but also of the Gentiles, and that it is the duty of His chosen people to bring the light of Divine revelation to them. Thus the book of Jonah is a rebuke of the exclusiveness of the Jews who held themselves aloof from, and considered themselves superior to the Gentiles. Because of its description of a prophet's preaching to the Gentiles, Jonah has been referred to as the missionary book of the Old Testament. The theme of the book may be summed up as follows: God's love for the Gentiles seen in His sending of a prophet to turn them to repentance.

Author. Jonah was a Galilean from the town of Gath-hepher, near Nazareth. The Pharisees in Christ's time evidently overlooked this when they asserted that no prophet ever came from Galilee

(John 7:52). He ministered to the Ten Tribes during the reign of Jeroboam II during whose reign he prophesied concerning the restoration of some Israelitish territory (2 Kings 14:25-27). When Elisha's ministry closed, his began. Jesus Himself bore witness to Jonah's personal existence, miraculous fate, and prophetical office (Matt. 12:40).

CONTENTS

I. Jonah's First Commission, His Disobedience and Its Results (Chs. 1, 2).

II. Jonah's Second Commission, His Obedience and Its Results (Ch. 3).

III. Jonah's Complaint and God's Answer (Ch. 4).

I. Jonah's First Commission, His Disobedience and Its Results (Chs. 1, 2).

1. Jonah's destination: Nineveh. Nineveh was the capital of the Assyrian empire, and at the time of Jonah, it was at the height of its pride and prosperity. It had a circumference of about 54 to 60 miles, and was surrounded by a wall a hundred feet high, so broad that three chariots could ride abreast on it. The population must have been about one million. The walled towns of Babylon seem to have enclosed large spaces for cultivation and pasture so that they were able to stand a prolonged siege. That Nineveh was a city of this kind is attested by the reference to its having "much cattle."

2. Jonah's disobedience. Many believe that Jonah's motive in disobeying God was a personal and selfish one—namely fear of being branded a false prophet, knowing as he did that God would spare the city if it repented, and its repentance would bring a result that would contradict his message of impending destruction. Others, however, do not believe this motive strong enough to

account for Jonah's flight from duty. They assert
that he was inspired by patriotism, though that
patriotism blinded him to mercy. Being a prophet
he knew that Assyria would some day invade the
land of Israel and practice on its inhabitants the
cruelties for which it was noted. Therefore he
chose rather to risk God's displeasure than to be
the means of preserving a nation that would bring
untold suffering on his people. John Urquhart, a
noted scholar, thus states the matter:

"Assyria had been laying her hand for some
generations upon the nations on the Mediterran-
ean coast, and it was the hand of a fierce and ferocious mastery. No considerations of pity were per-
mitted to stand in the way of Assyrian policy. It
could not afford to garrison its conquests and it
practiced a plan which largely dispensed with leav-
ing garrisons behind the Assyrian army. There was
unsparing slaughter to begin with. The kings
in their inscriptions seem to gloat over the spec-
tacle presented by the field of battle. They describe how it was covered by the corpses of the
vanquished. This carnage was followed by fiendish
inflictions on individual cities. The leading men, as
at Lachish when Sennacherib conquered that city,
were led forth, seized by the executioners and sub-
jected to various punishments, all of which were
filled to the brim with horror. Some of the victims
were held down while one of the band of torturers,
who are portrayed upon the monument gloat-
ing fiendishly over their fearful work, inserts his
hand into a victim's mouth, grips his tongue, and
wrenches it out by the roots. In another spot pegs
are driven into the ground. To these, another victim's wrists are fixed with cords. His ankles are
similarly made fast, and the man is stretched out
unable to move a muscle. The executioner then
applies himself to his task; and beginning at the
accustomed spot, the sharp knife makes its in-

cision, and the skin is raised inch by inch until the man is flayed alive. The skins are then stretched out upon the city walls, or otherwise disposed of, so as to terrify the people and leave behind long-enduring impressions of Assyrian vengeance. For others long sharp poles are prepared. The sufferer, taken, like the rest, from the leading men of the city, is laid down; the sharpened end of the pole is driven in through the lower part of the chest; the pole is then raised, bearing the writhing victim aloft; it is planted in the hole dug for it and the man is left to die.

"No man in Israel was ignorant of these things, Jonah may have witnessed them. Without doubt, too, Jonah knew that Assyria, the spoiler of the nations was the appointed executioner of God's vengeance on the ten tribes. . . . The word of the Lord came: Arise, go to Nineveh that great city and cry against it; for their wickedness is come up before me." Nineveh's cup, then, was full. Sentence was about to be pronounced. Gladder news than this, Jonah's ears had never heard. If Nineveh perished then Israel was saved! There was only one thing to be feared: God's mercy might arrest the smiting of God's justice. Jonah knew that Jehovah was a merciful God and that if Nineveh cried unto Him, Assyria might be saved, and then Israel would perish. But what if Nineveh were left without warning? What if she and her princes were now abandoned to reap the reward of their atrocities?

"It was a choice between vengeance on him, a rebellious prophet, and vengeance on his people. He would sacrifice himself, let Nineveh perish and so save Israel! This seems to have been Jonah's purpose and the reason for his sorrow at Nineveh's escape. Paul said he was willing to be accursed—cast out from God's presence—if by that means Israel could be saved. It was Christ's resolve when He saved us; for He was made a curse for us. The Lord told us that Jonah was a type of Himself. The type may have begun here."

Compare in this connection 2 Kings 8:7-13, where it is recorded that Elisha wept, when, looking into the future, he saw the atrocities that an invading army would perpetrate upon his people.

3. Jonah's punishment. No miracle in the Bible has evoked the unbelief of scientists and the ridicule of infidels as the story of Jonah's being swallowed by a whale. The main objection against the possibility of the miracle is the fact that it is claimed that the throat of the whale is not sufficiently wide to permit the passage of a man. From the standpoint of Scripture the miracle is an established fact, its veracity being confirmed by Christ (Matt. 12:40). The following quotations will show the possibility of the miracle from the natural standpoint:

"Any one who will read Frank Bullen's 'Cruise of the Cachalot' will have some idea of the size and habits of that mighty sea monster, the sperm whale. Mr. Bullen is an experienced whaler and speaks of what he has actually seen. He tells us in more places than one, how they caught whales of 'such gigantic proportions as over seventy feet long, with a breadth of bulk quite in proportion to such a vast length,' the head of which alone 'the skipper himself estimated to weigh fifteen tons!' And the idea of a whale's gullet being incapable of admitting any large substance, Mr. Bullen characterizes as 'a piece of crass ignorance.' He tells how on one occasion 'a shark fifteen feet in length has been found in the stomach of a sperm whale,' and adds this remarkable piece of evidence, 'that when dying the sperm whale **always ejects the contents of its stomach.'** He tells of one full-grown whale which has been caught and killed. 'the ejected food from whose stomach was in mass-

es of enormous size, larger than any we have yet
seen on the voyage, some of them being estimated
to be of the size of our hatch house'—viz., eight
feet by six feet by six feet. And yet we are asked
to believe that a whale could not swallow a man!"
—Sydney Collett: "All About the Bible."

The following is from the Springfield Leader,
Dec. 7, 1924. "The Rev. Dr. Straton, famous New
York fundamentalist, and the enemy of evolution,
believes that he has discovered a man, who actually—in modern times (1891)—suffered the same
fate as Jonah. This man James Bartley, able
British seaman and member of the whaling ship
Star of the East. In the attempt to capture a
gigantic sperm whale, in a whaling expedition off
the coast of Labrador, a whale upset one of the
boats. The men were saved by the other boat,
with the exception of two; these were thought to
have been drowned. They finally succeeded in kill-
ing the whale and towed it to the shore. Then
they proceeded to cut it up, and the second day
after it was captured, they opened the whale's
stomach, and to their amazement, found one of
their comrades, whom they thought drowned, unconscious but still alive. He suffered intensely
afterwards but finally made a complete recovery
after a long stay in a British hospital. Dr. Straton
says that the account was fully investigated by
one of the most careful, and painstaking journalists
of Europe, M. de Parville, editor of the Journal
des Debats, who said that the statements given by
the captain and the crew of the English vessel
coincided perfectly and were worthy of belief."

Note: Let the student make himself well acquainted with the above facts.

4. Jonah's prayer and deliverance (Ch. 2). In
his prayer Jonah quotes copiously from the Psalms.
He identifies himself with the saints of old, appro-

priating their experiences as recorded in the Word
of God. "There seems to be a strong probability
that Jonah actually did die and was raised from the
dead. If he actually did die, this only adds one
more to the resurrections recorded in the Bible and
makes Jonah a still more remarkable type of
Christ. To those who believe in God, there is no
difficulty in believing in the resurrection if sufficiently well attested."—Dr. Torrey.

III. Jonah's Second Commission, His Obedience, and Its Results (Chap. 3).

"To grasp the significance of the events in this
chapter it is necessary to know that the Ninevites
worshiped the fish-god, Dagon, part human and
part fish. They believed that he came out of the
sea and founded their nation, and that messengers
came to them from the sea from time to time. If
God, therefore, would send a preacher to them,
what more likely that He would bring His plan
down to their level and send a real messenger from
the sea? Doubtless great numbers saw Jonah cast
up from the sea and accompanied him to Nineveh
as his witnesses and credentials.

"There are two side arguments that corrobor-
ate the historicity of this event. In the first place,
'Oannes' is the name of one of the incarnations of
the fish-god, but this name with 'J' before it is
the spelling for Jonas in the New Testament. In
the second place, there was for centuries an Assyrian mound named 'Yunnas,' a corrupted Assyrian
form for Jonas, and it was this mound's name that
first gave the suggestion to the archaeologists that
the ancient city of Nineveh might be buried beneath it. Botta associated 'Yunnas' with Jonah,
and so pushed in his spade and struck the walls of
the city."—From Dr. Gray's Christian Worker's
Commentary.

In this chapter we shall answer three questions

asked by modern critics of the book of Jonah. The quotations are from Urquhart's New Biblical Guide.

1. Is it possible that a great heathen city like Nineveh should be so moved by the preaching of an obscure Hebrew preacher? In answer let it be noted that Jonah preached to them at a time when they were experiencing an alarming decline of power. There was possibly an expectation of coming calamity, and the presence of a prophet who had been thrown up by a fish would be sufficient to stir the superstitious people, who believed that their god sent messengers from the sea.

2. But was it at all likely that the state would interfere and a royal edict be issued enjoining a prolonged fast? Was action of this kind in accord with Assyrian custom? "It was just such a fast," says Professor Sayce, "as was ordained by Esarhaddon II, when the northern foe was gathering against the Assyrian empire, and prayers were raised to the sun-god to 'remove the sin' of the king and people. 'From this day,' runs the inscription, 'from the third day of the month even the month Iyyar, to the fifteenth day of Ab of this year, for these hundred days (and) hundred nights the prophets have proclaimed (a period of supplication).' The prophets of Nineveh had declared that it was necessary to appease the anger of heaven, and the king accordingly issued his proclamation enjoining the solemn service of humiliation for one hundred days."

3. Was it the Assyrian custom to cause even the beasts to share in the humiliation (Jonah 3:7)? "Herodotus has answered that question long ago. He tells us that, when the Persians were in Greece, a battle was fought in which a general, endeared to the whole army, was slain. 'On their arrival at the camp,' says Herodotus, 'the death of Masistius spread a general sorrow through the army, and greatly afflicted Mardonius himself. They cut off

the hair from themselves, **their horses, and their beasts of burden,** and all Boeotia resounded with their cries and lamentations. The man they had lost was, next to Mardonius, most esteemed by the Persians and their king. Thus the barbarians **in their manner** honored the deceased Masistius.'"

IV. Jonah's Complaint and God's Answer (Ch. 4).

Jonah still had a lingering hope that tne city might be destroyed (v. 5). He was still influenced by a misguided patriotism that had blinded him to mercy. God dealt gently with His servant and by an object lesson rebuked the petulant and vindictive spirit of the prophet. Jonah was willing to spare a worthless gourd yet was angry because God had spared a great city and its teeming population. If Jonah was willing to spare the gourd should not God spare Nineveh?

Micah

Theme. Micah prophesied about the same time as Isaiah, with whom he may have come into contact, since there are marked resemblances in their prophecies (i. e., compare Isa. 2:1-4 with Mic. 4:1-5). One has said that the prophecy of Isaiah is an enlargement of that of Micah. Like that of Isaiah the prophecy of Micah may be divided into two main sections: denunciatory (chs. 1-3) and consolatory (Chs. 4-7). In the first division the prophet presents a picture of a sinful nation doomed to captivity; in the second, of a redeemed people enjoying millennial blessings. In the first division he shows us Israel as misled and destroyed by false rulers; in the second, he presents us the same people restored by Messiah, the true Ruler. The theme may be summed up as follows: Israel, destroyed by false leaders, and saved by the true Leader, the Messiah.

Author. Micah was a native of Moresheth-gath, a village about 20 miles southwest of Jerusalem. He was a prophet from the country. "No prophet dated his birth from Jerusalem, though it was the city in which many witnessed and many were slain. Jerusalem killed the prophets but did not send them. They were sent from the mountain regions and rural towns." Micah prophesied during the reigns of Pekahiah, Pekah, and Hoshea over Israel, and of Jotham, Ahaz and Hezekiah over Judah (2 Kings 15:23-30). He had a message for both Judah and Israel, of which kingdoms he predicted the captivity. His largest work was done in the reign of Hezekiah who was deeply moved by his prophecies (Jer. 26:10-19). His prophecy of the destruction of Jerusalem was an indirect means of saving the life of Jeremiah when the latter was about to be put to death for making a similar prediction (Jer. 26:10-19).

CONTENTS

I. Denunciation (Chs. 1-3).
II. Consolation (Chs. 4-7).

I. Denunciation (Chs. 1 to 3).

1. Judgment upon Samaria for her incurable disposition to idolatry (1:1-8).

2. Judah has been affected by her sinfulness and has become involved in her guilt (1:9-16).

3. Because of the wickedness of rulers and people the nation will go into captivity (2:1-11). Yet there will be a restoration (vv. 12, 13).

4. A rebuke of the leaders of the people for their indifference to truth and righteousness, and for their mercenary motives (Ch. 3). A denunciation of (a) Civil rulers (vv. 1-4), (b) Prophets (vv. 5-10), (c) Priests (v. 11).

5. The nation will suffer for the sins of its leaders, for it evidently shares in their iniquity (v. 12; compare Jer. 5:31).

II. Consolation (Chs. 4 to 7).

1. Though Zion will be destroyed (3:12), yet in the last days it will be restored and exalted (4:1-8). (The following outline is suggested by Mr. Tucker.) Those days will witness—

(a) Universal administration. "The mountain of the house of the Lord shall be established in the top of the mountains."

(b) Universal visitation. "The people shall flow into it."

(c) Universal education. "He will teach us of His ways."

(d) Universal legislation. "The law shall go forth from Zion."

(e) Universal evangelization. "The word of the Lord from Jerusalem."

(f) Universal pacification. "Nation shall not lift up sword against nation."

(g) Universal adoration. "We will walk in the name of our God."

(h) Universal restoration. "And I will make her that halted a remnant; and her that was cast off a strong nation."

(i) Universal coronation. "And the Lord shall reign over them."

2. But this vision is for the future. For the present, there is dismay, helplessness and captivity (4:9, 10).

3. Yet ultimately Israel's enemies and captors will be punished (4:11-13).

4. Israel's trouble will last until the second coming of Messiah, their true ruler (5:1, 2). Foreordained from eternity to be Israel's Saviour, He is a pledge of Israel's deliverance from all their enemies and their final restoration (5:3-15).

5. Jehovah challenges His people to testify, if they can, if Jehovah ever did aught but acts of kindness to them from the earliest times of their

history—if they can produce any excuse for their forsaking Him (6:1-5).

6. They are religious, but their religion is a mere formality (6:6-7) that does not produce that practical righteousness which Jehovah requires (v. 8). Their conduct proves that they are keeping the statutes of Omri and works of Ahab—wicked kings of Israel (6:9-16).

7. The corruption of the nation is universal (7:1-6). It seems almost impossible to find a good man, an honest ruler, or a faithful friend. A man's enemies are those of his own household.

8. Yet there remains a faithful remnant, represented by the prophet, who lift up their voice in intercession for their nation (7:1-14). Their prayer is answered by Jehovah who promises restoration (vv. 15-17). Looking through the gloom of his own times, the prophet praises the faithful God who will yet restore Israel and purge them from their sins and thus fulfill the covenant made to the fathers (vv. 18-20).

CHAPTER XI

Nahum

Theme. The book of Nahum has but one outstanding theme; namely, the destruction of Nineveh. It is a sequel to the message of the prophet Jonah, by whose ministry, the Ninevites were lead to repentance and saved from impending doom. It is evident that they repented of their former repentance, and so gave themselves to idolatry, cruelty, and oppression, that one hundred and twenty years later, Nahum pronounced against them the judgment of God in the form of utter destruction. "Nahum's object was to inspire his countrymen, the Jews, with the assurance that, however alarming their position might seem, exposed to the attacks of the mighty Assyrian, who had already carried away the Ten Tribes, yet that not only should the Assyrian fail in his attack on Jerusalem (Isaiah Chs. 36, 37), but Nineveh his own capital would be taken and his empire overthrown; and this not by arbitrary exercise of Jehovah's power, but for the iniquities of the city and its people."

Author. Practically nothing is known concerning Nahum. He was a native of Elkosh, a village which some believe to have been in Galilee. He prophesied most during the early part of the reign of Josiah since he mentions the fall of No-Amon or Thebes (3:8) which occurred in the latter part of Manasseh's reign.

CONTENTS

I. Jehovah the Righteous Judge (Ch. 1).

Before describing the judgment of Nineveh, the prophet describes the judge, Jehovah, whom he shows to be, not an unjust, capricious executioner, but one who is slow to anger, who waits patiently for the fruits of repentance before punishing. "Nahum is the complement of Jonah. Jonah reveals the judgment on Nineveh **withdrawn,** and Nahum, the judgment on Nineveh **executed.** The Ninevites repented of their repentance described in Jonah, whereupon God repented of His mercy shown them at that time, and poured out His wrath on them. Of that wrath one says, 'The permanent value of the book is that it sets before the mind as no other book of the Old Testament, the picture of the wrath of God.' Do not let us imagine when we think of the anger of God, that it is anything like the hot, passionate, blind, foolish, blundering of a man in a temper. He is slow to anger; yet once having crossed over in the presence of things which demand a new attitude of vengeance, He is as irresistible as a hurricane that beats the sea into fury, or the simoom that sweeps the land with desolation. Note how the words, 'jealous, vengeance, wrath, anger, indignation, fierceness, fury,' describe the overwhelming fact of the anger of God. In man, wrath becomes his master, and drives him; God is always master of His wrath and uses it."

The following are the contents of this section:

1. The theme of the book: the burden of Nineveh (v. 1).

2. God is a jealous God visiting judgment on His adversaries, yet He is slow to anger, and in judgment remembers those that trust Him (vv. 2-8).

3. It is vain for the Assyrians to imagine that they can resist the Lord and destroy His people (vv. 9-11).

4. For God will surely deliver His own (vv. 12-14).

5. Because the Lord will deliver His people, they are to remain loyal to Him and to His service (v. 15).

II. Jehovah's Righteous Judgment (Chs. 2, 3).

"Nineveh, the destruction of which is foretold by the prophet, was at that time the capital of a great and flourishing empire. It was a city of vast extent and population, and was the center of the principal commerce of the world. Its wealth, however, was not altogether derived from trade. It was a 'bloody city,' 'full of lies and robbery' (3:1). It plundered the neighboring nations; and is compared by the prophet to a family of lions, which 'fill their holes with prey, and their dens with ravin' (2:11, 12). At the same time it was strongly fortified: its colossal walls are said by Diodorus Siculus to have been a hundred feet high, and wide enough on the summit for three chariots to be driven abreast on them; with fifteen hundred towers bidding defiance to all enemies. Yet, so totally was it destroyed, that, in the second century after Christ, not a vestige remained of it; and its very site was long a matter of uncertainty."— Angus-Green.

"Extensive excavations and marvelous discoveries have of late years been made in the mounds of Nineveh. Botta began his labors in 1842; Layard, in 1845; Rassam, in 1852; and Loftus, in 1854. The results of their researches as to extent, character, and variety of marbles, sculptures, and inscriptions, brought to light, have confounded cavilers at the sacred Scriptures, entranced with delight antiquaries and archaeologists, and astonished the whole world."

The following is the contents of this section:
1. The siege and capture of the city (2:1-13).

2. The sins of the city (3:1-7).

3. Her doom will be as sure as that of the Egyptian city of No-Amon, a city that was once populous and powerful (3:8-19).

Habakkuk

Theme. The book of Habakkuk presents a picture of a man of God, perplexed by the problem of the seeming toleration of evil on the part of the Lord. The prophet is surrounded on every hand by wickedness unpunished and triumphant. At first his cry for judgment is apparently unheeded by God. When his prayer is at last answered and judgment pronounced, he is further perplexed that the agents of God's judgments, the Chaldeans, are more wicked and more worthy of punishment than the victims. Habakkuk is full of doubt and questionings. But happily he takes his perplexities to the Lord who quickly dispells them, and who presents a solution to his problems summed up in a statement which is the heart of the book—"The just shall live by his faith" (2:4). That is, no matter how gloomy the outlook and how triumphant evil may seem, the just man must not judge by appearances, but rather by God's Word; though the wicked may live and prosper in their wickedness and the righteous suffer, the latter are to live a life of faithfulness and trustfulness. The prophet learned this lesson well, for, whereas his prophecy begins with mystery, questioning and doubt, it ends with certainty, affirmation, and faith. We shall sum up the theme as follows: The conflict and ultimate triumph of faith.

Author. Practically nothing is known of Habakkuk save what may be learned from conflicting traditions. From 3:1, 19, it has been inferred that he was a Levite, and participated in the music of the temple. As Nahum predicted the destruction of the Assyrian nation, and Obadiah, of the Edomite, so Habakkuk prophesied of the downfall of the Chaldean empire. Since he speaks of the growing power of the last-named nation and of the imminence of their invasion of Judah, it has been concluded that Habakkuk prophesied during the reigns of Jehoahaz and Jehoiakim.

CONTENTS

I. The Conflict of Faith (Chs. 1, 2).
II. The Triumph of Faith (Ch. 3).

I. The Conflict of Faith (Chs. 1, 2).

1. Habakkuk's first conflict (1:1-4). The prophet sees evil and violence on every side, the law violated, and the righteous persecuted. He cries out to the Lord to visit judgment on Judah because of this condition, but seemingly his cry is unheeded. He pours forth his perplexity in these words: "O Lord, how long shall I cry and thou wilt not hear! even cry out to thee of violence, and thou wilt not save!"

2. Jehovah's first answer (1:5-11). Though it may sometimes appear that Jehovah is silent and indifferent, yet He is working. In due time He will visit judgment upon wicked Judah, using as His agents the terrible Chaldeans.

3. The prophet's second conflict (1:12 to 2:1). The first problem is solved; God will punish the evil doers in Zion, by bringing upon them the fierce Chaldeans. But this solution suggests another problem to Habakkuk. Viewing the pride, false confidence, and destructiveness of the invaders, he cannot understand why God should punish His people by a nation less righteous than they (1:13). Though the Lord has ordained the Chaldeans to judge His people (1:12), can it be the will of Him who is too pure to behold iniquity (v. 13), to allow that nation to trample as reckless-

ly upon Judah as upon the other nations (vv. 14-17)?

4. Jehovah's second answer (2:2-5). Though the Chaldeans have been commissioned to execute judgment on Judah, yet, in their arrogant pride they have exceeded their commission (2:4, first part). Though the wicked, as represented by the Chaldeans, may prosper in his iniquity, and the righteous suffer, yet the latter is to live by a life of faithfulness to Jehovah, a life inspired by faith in His promises and justice (2:4, second part). Though Jehovah will use the Chaldeans as a scourge upon His people, yet the former shall not go unpunished (vv. 5-20). The prophet is to write this prophecy of the Chaldeans' ultimate overthrow and post it where all may read (2:2). Though its fulfillment may be delayed, the righteous are to wait patiently for it, trusting in Jehovah's word (2:3).

II.   The Triumph of Faith (Ch. 3).

The following are the contents of this section:

1. At first the prophet was wondering why Jehovah seemed to delay judgment on the wicked of His people (1:2-3). Now he has heard the Lord's sentence, he is afraid and prays that He may repeat on behalf of His people His work of deliverance as of old, and that He may remember mercy in the midst of judgment (3:1, 2).

2. He presents a vivid picture of Jehovah's going forth in the days of old to save His people, the implication being that His past mercies to Israel are a pledge of His future mercies toward them (vv. 3-16).

3. Habakkuk has learned his lesson of faith. Whatever be his circumstances or that of his people, however dark and hopeless the outlook, he will rejoice in the Lord, the God of his salvation (vv. 17-19).

Zephaniah

Theme. The frequent recurrence of the phrase "the day of the Lord," will suggest immediately that Zephaniah has a message of judgment. But in common with most of the other prophets, he has also a message of restoration. "It has been said that this prophecy of Zephaniah is peculiarly desert and barren—no life, no flower, no fruit, none of the beauties of nature; nothing but a world swept by a simoom. If this is so, what is the reason of it? Look at the conditions described. Men settled on their lees in luxury denying the interference of God. A city that did not obey His voice, received not correction, did not trust in the Lord, did not draw near to God. Men and city materialized, self-centered, luxurious; the rulers, princes, judges, prophets, and priests alike corrupt. The whole condition may be expressed in one word—chaos. What, then, is the story of 'the day of the Lord'? That of chaos consumed, disorder disorganized, evil conditions destroyed, until the city appears before the eye of the astonished prophet as a simoom-swept landscape with never a blade of grass. . . . A modern expositor has said that it is perfectly patent that this last chapter (ch. 3) was not written by Zephaniah, because the contrast is too great between the picture of the awful, sweeping, irrevocable judgment, and that of the restoration. No one can imagine, he declares, that the same man wrote both. All of which is the result of the expositor's blindness. The last picture is that of the enthroned Jehovah, the picture of a new order; songs instead of sorrow, service instead of selfishness, solidarity instead of scattering. That is the intent of judgment. . . . The very contrast demonstrates the unity of authorship."—Campbell Morgan. We shall sum up the theme as follows: The night of judgment on

Israel and the nations, followed by the morning of restoration for the former, and conversion for the latter.

Author. Contrary to common usage, Zephaniah carries his descent back to His great-great-grandfather, Hizkiah (Hezekiah). Some believe that this fact indicates that either he was descended from Hezekiah or that he was of noble descent. He prophesied during the reign of Josiah, king of Judah. In the period between the cessation of the prophecies of Isaiah, Micah, and Nahum, and the days of Zephaniah and Jeremiah, there was a period of 55 years, during which the wicked Manasseh reigned (2 Chron. 33:1-20), and during which the spirit of prophecy was dormant. It revived during the reign of Josiah (2 Chron. Chs. 34, 35) when that monarch began the great reformation, in which Zephaniah probably played an important part (compare 2 Chron. 34:4, 5 and Zeph. 1:4, 5).

CONTENTS
I.   A Warning of Judgment (Ch. 1).
II. A Call to Repentance (2:1 to 3:7).
III. A Promise of Restoration (3:8-20).

I. A Warning of Judgment (Ch. 1).

Note the contents of this chapter:

1. A sweeping, destructive judgment announced (vv. 1-3).

2. A prophecy of the overthrow of idolatry (vv. 4-6). Fulfilled in Josiah's reign.

3. The coming punishment of Judah is set forth under the figure of a sacrifice, the victims representing the people, and the guests, the Chaldean invaders (v. 7).

4. The judgment will fall on all classes: on the rulers and their children (v. 8); on their servants who plunder the people (v. 9); on the merchants

(vv. 10, 11); on those who live in luxury, indifference and skepticism (vv. 12, 13).

5. A description of the day of Jehovah, the day of His vengeance on the guilty (vv. 14-18).

II. A Call to Repentance (Chs. 2:1 to 3:7).

1. A warning to the wicked to repent in order to escape judgment (2:1, 2).

2. An exhortation to the just to persevere in meekness and righteousness in order that they may be hid in that day (2:3).

3. This call to repentance enforced by the certainty of judgments on the surrounding nations (2:4-15).

4. Jerusalem shall not escape, for she has failed to heed the warning conveyed by the fate of those nations whom Jehovah had punished (3:1-7).

III. A Promise of Restoration (Ch. 3:8-20).

The following are the contents of this section:
1. The judgment of the nations, in the last days, will be followed by their conversion and the institution of the universal worship of Jehovah (vv. 8, 9).

2. Jehovah will purge from Israel those who reposed in a self-righteous pride of their covenant privileges; and purged from these sinners, Israel will be a humble, trustful and holy nation (vv. 12, 13).

3. Jehovah will lift His chastening hand from Israel, will bless the remnant, punish Israel's enemies and will dwell in the midst of a restored and exalted nation (vv. 14-20).

CHAPTER XII

Haggai

Haggai is the first of the prophets known as the post-Exilic; i. e., prophesying after the captivity. Zechariah and Malachi are the other two. Read Ezra Chs. 1-7 for the historical background of this prophecy.

Theme. Under the favorable decree of Cyrus, the Jewish remnant returned to their land under the leadership of Zerubbabel, their governor, and Joshua, their high priest. After settling in the land, the people set up an altar of burnt offerings on the site of the temple. Two years later amid great rejoicings, the foundations of the temple were laid. Their rejoicing soon turned into sadness, for, through the efforts of the hostile Samaritans, the work was ordered discontinued by an imperial decree. For sixteen years the temple remained unfinished until the reign of Darius, when that king issued an order permitting its completion. But in the meantime the people had become indifferent and selfish, and instead of building the temple, they were occupied with the beautifying of their own homes. As a result of this negligence, they were punished with drought and barrenness. Their enquiry concerning the reason for these calamities gave Haggai the occasion for his message, in which he declared that the people's selfish indifference in regard to the needs of the temple was the cause of their misfortunes. We shall sum up the theme as follows: The result of the neglect of the temple's completion—divine displeasure and punishment; the result of the temple's completion —divine blessing and promises of future glory.

100

Author. Little is known of the personal history of Haggai, "the prophet of the second temple," except that he prophesied after the captivity and that his mission was to encourage the people in the rebuilding of the temple. "Haggai's work was intensely practical and important. Jehovah employed him to awaken the conscience and stimulate the enthusiasm of his compatriots in the rebuilding of the temple. No prophet ever appeared at a more critical juncture in the history of the people, and, it may be added, no prophet was more successful."

CONTENTS

The book divides itself naturally into four distinctly mentioned messages:

I. First message: the neglect of the second temple's completion (1:1-15).

II. Second message: the glory of the second temple (2:1-9).

III. Third message: sacrifice without obedience (to rebuild the temple) will not sanctify (2:10-19).

IV. Fourth message: the safety and perpetuity of the house of Israel (2:20-23).

I. First message: the neglect of the second temple's completion (Ch. 1:1-15).

1. The excuse for the neglect (vv. 1, 2). "The time is not come that the Lord's house should be built." The people were probably waiting for some special revelation from God before they would perform what they knew to be their duty.

2. The cause of the neglect—the people's selfishness (vv. 3, 4). They did not wait for any special command to build and embellish their own homes.

3. The punishment for the neglect—drought and barrenness (vv. 5-11).

4. The repentance for the neglect (vv. 12-15). The people set to work on the temple.

II. The second message: the glory of the second temple (Ch. 2:1-9).

1. The people's discouragement (vv. 1-3). Remembering the magnificence of Solomon's temple, the people were evidently discouraged by the thought that the present temple would not equal it in beauty and glory. They knew that it would lack the Shekinah glory that filled the first temple.

2. The Divine encouragement (vv. 4-9). The glory of the second temple will be greater than that of the first, declares Jehovah, for Messiah Himself, the Lord of glory, will enter it. This was fulfilled at Christ's first coming when He entered the temple (John 2:13-25; compare Malachi 3:1). There may be a more complete fulfillment at His second coming.

III. Third message: sacrifices without obedience (to rebuild the temple) will not sanctify (Ch. 2:10-19).

1. A parable (vv. 10-14). The lesson contained in these scriptures is as follows: holiness is not contagious, but evil is. The sacrifices offered on the altar were not sufficient to sanctify a land which the disobedience of the people had polluted. Therefore the land was barren. "The faint aroma of sanctity coming from the altar was too feeble to pervade the secular atmosphere of their lives. Haggai argues that Israel's sacrifices for sixteen years had been unclean in God's sight, and had brought them no blessing, because the temple was in ruins."

2. A warning (vv. 15-18). The blight upon the land was caused by disobedience.

3. A promise (v. 19). Now that the people have set themselves to the work in earnest, the Lord will bless them.

IV. Fourth message: the safety and perpetuity of the house of Israel (Ch. 2:20-23).

1. The coming world commotions (2:20-22). Comparing Haggai 2:6, 7 and Hebrews 12:26-28, we see here a reference to the final world upheaval preceding Christ's second coming.

2. The assurance of safety (v. 23). The national disturbances in Zerubbabel's time had perhaps made him fear for the safety of his nation. As a representative of the house of David and an ancestor of the Messiah, he receives a promise of protection and safety for himself and his people. All the nations of the world shall be shaken, but the Jewish nation under Messiah, of whom Zerubbabel is a type, shall be established.

Zechariah

Theme. The historical background of the prophecy of Zechariah is the same as that of Haggai, both prophets ministering during the same period and having a similar mission. Zechariah's mission was to encourage by the promise of present success and future glory, the Jewish remnant, who were disheartened by present distresses and who were slow to rebuild their temple. The people had good reasons for being discouraged. They had once been a free nation, having king and constitution. But now they had returned to a country under foreign rule, to a country without a king, and stripped of power. Their present condition presented a dark picture, but Zechariah made this serve as a dark background of a more glorious scene, as he, by a series of visions and prophecies, depicted a restored Jerusalem protected and indwelt by the Messiah, and capital of a nation exalted above all others. Besides the promise of future glory, the prophet gave promises of present success and achievement, for he assured the remnant that their temple would be rebuilt in spite of opposition. But Zechariah could offer no permanent encouragement short of the promise of Messiah's coming. Israel's present experience is but a foreshadowing of their future experience. As it was through the chastisement of the Babylonish captivity that the nation was purged of the sin of idolatry, so it will be by the fires of the great tribulation that Israel will be purified from its sin of sins—the rejection of its Messiah and King (13:8, 9; 12:10; 13:1). We shall sum up the theme as follows: An encouragement to the nation to serve their God faithfully through present distress, in view of the future glories of the times of the Messiah.

Author. Zechariah was probably born in Babylon. He entered the ministry while yet a young man (2:4), and began prophesying a short time later than Haggai, whose colleague he was. His mission was to stir up the flagging zeal of the people and encourage them by taking their eyes off the dark present and directing them to the bright future.

CONTENTS

We shall divide the book into the following three sections:

I.   Symbolical: Visions of Hope (Chs. 1-6).
II. Practical: Exhortations to Obedience and Piety (Chs. 7, 8).
III. Prophetical: Promises of Glory through Tribulation (Chs. 9-14).

I. Symbolical: Visions of Hope (Chaps. 1 to 6).

Chapter 1:1-6 forms the introduction to the book. The remnant are admonished to take warning from the fate of their fathers, who disobeyed the voice of the prophets, and suffered in consequence. The people are to obey the message of the present prophets, Haggai and Zechariah, whose words will be fulfilled as surely as those of the former prophets.

Then follows a series of visions conveying messages of God's care and protection of His people.

1. The vision of the rider among the myrtle trees (1:7-17). The rider who, together with the horses represents God's agents in the earth, informs the angel of the Lord that the whole world is at rest and still, thus symbolizing that the time had come for the fulfillment of God's promises in relation to Israel's restoration. In response to the angel's intercession, Jehovah says that He is displeased with the heathen who have exceeded their commission in regard to punishing Israel. He will return and rebuild the cities of Judah.

2. The vision of the four horns and the four carpenters (1:18-21), teaching the destruction of those who are Israel's oppressors.

3. The vision of the man with the measuring line (Ch. 2), symbolizing the rebuilding of Jerusalem. It will be rebuilt without walls because of the coming increase in population and because Jehovah Himself will be as a wall of fire round about her.

4. The vision of Joshua the high priest (Ch. 3). The high priest, divested of his filthy garments, and reclothed with clean raiment, typifies the cleansing of the Jewish remnant, whose representative he is (vv. 1-7). Joshua and his fellow priests are a type of the Messiah, who will effect the final purification of Israel (vv. 8-10).

5. The vision of the golden candlestick and the olive trees (Ch. 4). By the Spirit working through Zerubbabel and Joshua (the two olive trees), will the rebuilding of the temple (the golden candlestick) and the restoration of the nation be effected, and not by human power (v. 6).

6. The vision of the flying roll (5:1-4), teach-

ing that after the completion of the temple, God will punish those violating His laws.

7. The vision of the ephah (5:5-11). The teaching of this vision seems to be as follows: Israel's sins will be removed—especially the sins of idolatry and rebellion—and they will be carried to Babylon, the center of idolatry and the scene of the first rebellion, and probably the scene of the final apostasy and rebellion.

8. The vision of the four chariots (6:1-8), teaching the swiftness and extent of Jehovah's judgments against Israel's former oppressors.

9. The symbolic crowning of Joshua, the high priest (6:9-15), typifying the crowning of the Messiah as King-priest, and the building of His spiritual temple in which He shall be enthroned as ruler and intercessor.

II. Practical: Exhortations to Obedience and Piety (Chaps. 7, 8).

The above exhortations were partly occasioned by the enquiry of representatives of the people as to whether they should continue to fast in commemoration of the fall of Jerusalem (7:1-3). The following lessons are contained in the prophet's answer:

1. God desires obedience rather than fasting. It was the disobedience of the people that brought on the judgments that were the occasion for the fasts (Ch. 7).

2. When the cause of fasting and mourning—sin—is removed, then Israel's fasts will be turned into feasts (8:19). That day is coming, for Israel will be finally regathered and Jerusalem will become the religious center of the earth (Ch. 8).

III. Prophetical: Promises of Glory through Tribulation (Chs. 9 to 14).

Following Dr. Gray's suggestion, we shall divide this section according to the periods of Israel's history: Israel under Grecian rule (Chs. 9-10); Israel under Roman rule (Ch. 11); Israel under Messiah's rule (Chs. 12-14).

1. Israel under Grecian rule (Chs. 9, 10).

(a) A prophecy concerning the conquests of Alexander, emperor of Greece, a king who lived about three hundred years before Christ (9:1-8). Verses 1-7 record his conquests along the west coast of Palestine; and verse 8, the deliverance of Jerusalem out of his hands. Josephus, the Jewish historian, gives us an account of the last-named event. He tells us that, after the conquest of Tyre and Gaza (mentioned in 9:1-7), Alexander set out for Jerusalem to punish Jaddus, the high priest, who had refused to submit to him. The Lord in a dream commanded Jaddus to open the gates to the conqueror, and dressed in his high-priestly garments, and attended by his priests, to receive Alexander in triumph. Jaddus obeyed, and Alexander, seeing this imposing procession, saluted the high priest and adored the God whose name was on the golden plate attached to the priest's headgear. Alexander then explained that, while in Macedonia, he had had a vision of this procession, and this vision had been brought to his mind by what he had just seen. He afterwards treated the Jews with great kindness.

(b) The coming of Messiah, who in contrast to Alexander, is the true King and world conqueror (9:9-12).

(c) A prophecy of the defeat of Antiochus Epiphanes, king of Syria (about 165 B. C.), one of the divisions of Alexander's empire (9:13-17). Antiochus, seeing that the Jews' religion stood in the way of their perfect submission to him conceived the plan of abolishing it and substituting the cults of Greece. He captured Jerusalem, defiled the temple, and interdicted the worship of Jehovah. Persecution ensued and continued until Judas Maccabeus and his brothers, the sons of the high priest placed themselves at the head of a Jewish army that drove the Syrians from the land. We may look upon this deliverance as the foreshadowing of Israel's final deliverance (Ch. 10).

2. Israel under Roman rule (Ch. 11). This chapter deals mainly with the rejection of the Messiah and the judgments following. Many of the predictions were through symbolic actions, such as the breaking of the staffs, etc. (vv. 10, 14). Taking this entire chapter as Messianic, we shall note as its contents:

(a) A picture of judgment, probably the one following Christ's rejection (vv. 1-6).

(b) Messiah's ministry—that of a Shepherd to Israel (vv. 7, 8).

(c) Messiah's rejection by the flock (vv. 9-11).

(d) Messiah's valuation by His people—thirty pieces of silver, the price of a slave (vv. 12, 13; compare Matt. 26:14-16; 27:3-10).

(e) The rejection of the true shepherd followed by the rise of a false shepherd—a type of Antichrist (vv. 15-17).

3. Israel under Messiah's rule (Chs. 12-14).

(a) The siege of Jerusalem and her deliverance by the appearance of Christ (Ch. 12).

(b) The purification of Israel (Ch. 13).

(c) The exaltation of Israel (Ch. 14).

Malachi

Theme. In Nehemiah we read the last page of Old Testament history; in the book of the prophet Malachi, Nehemiah's contemporary, we read the last page of Old Testament prophecy. Malachi, the last of the prophets, testifies, as do his predecessors, to the sad fact that Israel has failed. He presents us a picture of a people outwardly religious, but inwardly indifferent and insincere, a people to whom the service of Jehovah has become an empty formality, performed by a corrupt priesthood whom they did not respect. Under the ministry of Haggai and Zechariah the people were willing to acknowledge their faults and make amends; but now, so hardened have they become, that to the charges of Jehovah they offer insolent denials (1:1, 2; 2:17; 3:7). Worse still, many profess a skepticism as to the existence of a God of judgment, and others question the value of serving the Lord (2:17; 3:14, 15). As a ray of light shining upon this dark scene is the promise of the advent of the Messiah, who will come to the deliverance of the faithful remnant and to the judgment of the nation. The book closes with a prophecy of the coming of Elijah, Messiah's forerunner, and then the curtain drops on Old Testament revelation, not to be lifted again until four hundred years later, when the angel of Jehovah announces the coming of Him who is to go before the coming One in spirit and power of Elijah (Luke 1:17). We shall sum up the theme as follows: the last prophecy of the Old Testament, a revelation of a rebellious and insincere people, of a loyal remnant, and of a coming Messiah who will judge and purify the nation.

Notice the recurrence of the word "wherein" (See, e. g., 1, 2), which expresses the defiant attitude of the people in regard to Jehovah's accusations.

Author. Of the personal history of Malachi nothing is known. It is believed that he prophesied during the time of Nehemiah and supported him, as Haggai and Zechariah supported Zerubbabel. "The book of Malachi fits the situation round which Nehemiah worked as snugly as a bone fits a socket." The prophet denounced the very evils that existed in Nehemiah's time (Compare Neh. 13:10-12 and Mal. 3:8-10; Neh. 13:29 and Mal. 2:4-8; Neh. 13:23-27 and Mal. 2:10-16). He wrote so much about Christ that one has said, "Old Testament prophecy expired with the Gospel on its tongue."

CONTENTS

I. Warning and Rebuke: Messages to the Rebellious (Chs. 1:1 to 3:15).

1. A message to the whole nation (1:1-5)—His love for them, and their ingratitude. The people insolently question Jehovah's love for them, evidently thinking of their past afflictions, but forgetting that these were the chastenings of the Almighty to purify them. As a proof of His love to the nation, the Lord points to His gratuitous election of their father Jacob and the rejection of his brother. (Note the word "hate," does not signify hatred in the sense that we now understand it, but is here used in the sense of rejecting. Compare Luke 14:26 and Matt. 10:37 where the word "hate" means to love with a lesser affection). Edom is forever rejected of God and will be forever desolate. But Israel, forever chosen of God, will live to see Edom's desolation, and will gorify God's grace and love (vv. 4, 5).

2. Messages to the priests (1:6 to 2:9). The following sins are rebuked:

(a) Lack of reverence for the Lord (1:6). Note the spirit of self-satisfied insensibility to sin, revealed in the reply of the priests: "Wherein have we despised thee?" This attitude is manifest in all of the answers of people and priests to Jehovah's reproofs.

(b) The offering of blemished sacrifices (1:7-12). Darius and his successors had probably liberally supplied the priests with victims for the

sacrifices (Ezra 6:8-10), yet they presented none
but the worst. They offered to the Lord that
which they would not have dared to offer to their
governor (v. 8). But though polluted sacrifices are
offered in Palestine, yet among the heathen there
are and will be those who will bring a pure offering before the Lord (v. 11).

(c) The performing of God's service in the
spirit of indifference and discontent (1:11, 12).
They regarded God's service as irksome, and dis-
honored it by presenting the most worthless offerings.

(d) The violation of the Levitical covenant
(2:1-9). The Lord mentions those qualities that
the covenant required in a priest; namely, a close
walk with Jehovah, zeal to turn many from iniquity, and ability to teach (vv. 5-7). In all these
qualities the priesthood of Malachi's time were
sadly lacking (v. 8).

3. Messages to the people (2:11 to 3:15). The
following sins are rebuked:

(a) Sins of the family (2:10-16). Many of the
people had divorced their Israelitish wives in order
to marry foreign women (Compare Nehemiah
13:23-28).

(b) Skepticism (2:17). This verse forms the
transition to 3:1. The skeptics of the day were
insinuating that God delighted in evil-doers since
the latter seemed to prosper. Then, if that was
the case, why should they serve God (3:14, 15)?
Where is the God of judgment, they ask. The answer is forthcoming (3:1-6). The Lord whom they
seek (3:1) (whom they challenge to appear) will
come suddenly (when they least expect it) to His
temple and will visit judgment on priests and people. Not because Jehovah had changed was
judgment delayed, but because He had not changed
in regard to His covenant promises and because of
His unchanging mercy (v. 6).

(c) The withholding of the tithe (3:7-12; compare Nehemiah 13:10-14).

II. Predictions and Promises: Messages to the Faithful (Chs. 3:16 to 4:6).

1. A message to the righteous (3:16 to 4:3). In the darkest days of Israel's apostasy there has always been a remnant that have remained faithful to God. In Malachi's day, when the fire of religion was burning low, these faithful ones gathered to keep the holy flame alive. As the kings of Persia kept a record of those who had rendered them service, so that they might reward them (Esther 2:23; 6:1, 2; Ezra 4:5), so God is keeping His record (v. 16). These loyal ones are His jewels, His own peculiar treasure, whom He will preserve from the day of tribulation. In that day both the righteous and the wicked will be recompensed, and then will be silenced the skeptic's sneer (v. 18, compare 2:17; 3:14, 15). The Sun of righteousness will rise, to burn the wicked, but to shed healing rays upon the righteous (4:1-3).

2. The last exhortation of the Old Testament (4:4): "Remember ye the law of Moses." Until Messiah came revelation was to cease temporarily. The people are to remember the law, for, in the absence of the living prophets they are likely to forget it. The law is to be their rule of life and conduct during the four hundred years of silence intervening between the last Old Testament prophet and the coming of the Prophet of prophets.

3. The last prophecy of the Old Testament (4:5, 6). Before the coming of the great day of wrath, God will send the forerunner of the Messiah, Elijah, who will prepare the people for His coming. This prophecy was fulfilled in John the Baptist (Luke 1:17; Matt. 11:14; 17:11, 12). That it will have a future fulfillment is probable, for as the Messiah had a forerunner at His first advent, so He may have one at His second.